Approaches
to
Meditation

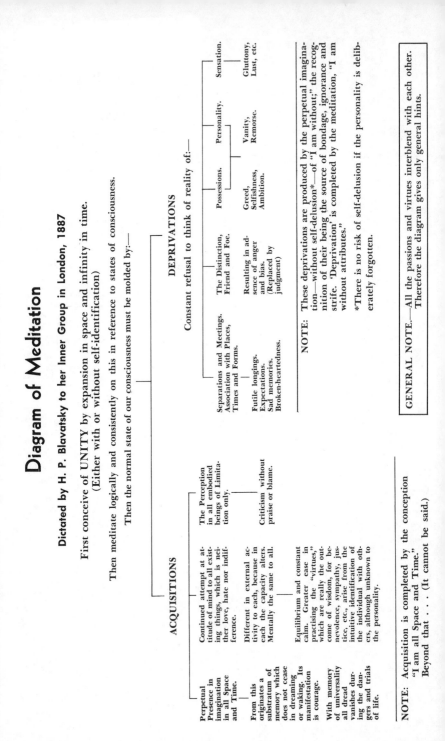

Diagram of Meditation

Dictated by H. P. Blavatsky to her Inner Group in London, 1887

First conceive of UNITY by expansion in space and infinity in time.
(Either with or without self-identification)

Then meditate logically and consistently on this in reference to states of consciousness.

Then the normal state of our consciousness must be molded by:—

ACQUISITIONS

- Perpetual Presence in imagination in all Space and Time.
- From this originates a substratum of memory which does not cease in dreaming or waking. Its manifestation is courage.
- With memory of universality all dread vanishes during the dangers and trials of life.

- Continued attempt at attitude of mind to all existing things, which is neither love, hate nor indifference.
- Different in external activity to each, because in each the capacity alters. Mentally the same to all.
- Equilibrium and constant calm. Greater ease in practising the "virtues," which are really the outcome of wisdom, for benevolence, sympathy, justice, etc., arise from the intuitive identification of the individual with others, although unknown to the personality.

- The Perception in all embodied beings of Limitation only.
- Criticism without praise or blame.

NOTE: Acquisition is completed by the conception "I am all Space and Time." Beyond that . . . (It cannot be said.)

DEPRIVATIONS

Constant refusal to think of reality of:—

Separations and Meetings. Association with Places, Times and Forms.	The Distinction, Friend and Foe.	Possessions.	Personality.	Sensation.
Futile longings. Expectations. Sad memories. Broken-heartedness.	Resulting in absence of anger and bias. (Replaced by judgment)	Greed, Selfishness, Ambition.	Vanity, Remorse.	Gluttony, Lust, etc.

NOTE: These deprivations are produced by the perpetual imagination—without self-delusion*—of "I am without;" the recognition of their being the source of bondage, ignorance and strife. "Deprivation" is completed by the meditation, "I am without attributes."

*There is no risk of self-delusion if the personality is deliberately forgotten.

GENERAL NOTE.—All the passions and virtues interblend with each other. Therefore the diagram gives only general hints.

Approaches
to
Meditation

Edited by
Virginia Hanson

A QUEST BOOK
Published under a grant from The Kern Foundation

THE THEOSOPHICAL PUBLISHING HOUSE
Wheaton, Ill,. U.S.A.

Madras, India / London, England

Original Quest Book edition published by the Theosophical Publishing House, Wheaton, Illinois, a department of The Theosophical Society in America

Second Quest book printing, 1976

Meditation.

   (A Quest book)
   Running title: Approaches to meditation.
   "First published as a special issue of the journal the American theosophist."
   Includes bibliographical references.
   1. Meditation. I. Hanson, Virginia, ed. II. The American theosophist (Wheaton, Ill.) III. Title: Approaches to meditation.

[BL627.M37]   248'.3   73-80

ISBN 0-8356-0436-5

CONTENTS

Chapter   **Page**

Introduction

Meditation: The Art of Being

JOY MILLS

Current popular interest in meditation has led to a proliferation of textbooks and manuals on the subject, ranging all the way from simple presentations promising the devotee almost instant enlightenment to extremely complex restatements of ancient disciplines frightening to the beginning aspirant. Often the very word itself conjures up pictures of the solitary individual seated in the lotus posture, eyes closed, a smile of utter tranquility upon his face, oblivious of all outer events, or of groups of wild-eyed young people, sitting in incense-filled rooms, chanting Sanskrit incantations. Neither picture, of course, is an accurate view of meditation, although the act of meditation may occur anytime, anywhere, alone or in a crowd. What is important is not the place or the posture, but rather a certain habitual attitude, or what one writer has called "the disposition of the soul."

For meditation, which the Quaker writer Bradford Smith defined as the "inward art," has to do with oneself, with the self one is or the self one hopes to become. A study of all the techniques in the world, an examination of meditation systems of the eastern and western religions and philosophies, a reading of texts and manuals, however authoritative, will not constitute the act of meditation or induce the meditative spirit. One brings only oneself to the act, whether one is alone or in a group. Whatever discipline is chosen, one is on one's own. A journey may be undertaken in many ways, but the choice of the conveyance is a very personal one and, when it is made, there are certain inevitable consequences. Some people just do not wish to fly; others will do anything to avoid walking, even to the corner drugstore. But when the decision has been to walk, little is gained by complaining that the road has a lot of rocks in it to bruise one's feet.

Since each brings only himself to the journey whatever conveyance is chosen, it is useful to look at the self one has brought. For our view of ourselves will have a great deal to do with what happens to us on the trip, as well as with the kind of journey we undertake. When someone asks, "Why meditate?" the only answer really is, "Because I want to." Of course, there may be an infinite number of factors involved in this "wanting," which is the decision reached by a consciousness called "I" but ultimately all of these factors coalesce in the moment when we say (whether to ourselves or to others does not matter): "I intend to meditate." We may have reasoned in advance that meditation is good for us, that it will lead to certain insights (or we hope it will), that it seems to have benefited others, and that, in any event, it is not likely to cost us very much in time or energy. Or we may act upon a conviction that there is beyond all the ephemeral and phenomenal paraphernalia of the external world a realm of reality which can be known and experienced, that this realm of reality holds within it all the causes from which the phenomenal is born, while yet remaining impartable and unitary, and further, that there is, therefore, a consciousness or the possibility of a consciousness which can embrace that realm.

THE ART OF BEING

The intention to meditate, then, precedes the act, but meditation is less an act than an art; it is not performance, but awareness. We may *do* a great many things, whether that doing be physical (such as the postures of some schools of meditative yoga) or mental (such as exercising the mind by concentration, imagination, etc.) ; whatever we do has a bearing upon our meditation, but only when one comes to oneself, in the totality of the Self, has one engaged in meditation. Perhaps the paradox is that we are then no longer aware that we are meditating; we simply *are*. In such a state of awareness, one does not say, "See, I am meditating." One is oneself, wholly, purely, without division. So meditation is not merely the harnessing of one's mind, although the mental processes may need to be reined in, controlled, directed; it is not just the stilling of emotional reactions (and how really easy it is to sit quietly, in solitude, and feel good will; the test, as always, is whether we can be equally serene in the midst of a storm!) ; it is not only the relaxation of the physical vehicle, so that for a time at least it does not intrude itself upon our attention. All of these tasks may prepare us for meditation, may be helps along the way, may be essential if we are to get on with the discovery of ourselves. Meditation is the art of being, an art to be practiced everywhere, continuously, whether alone or with others. And if one were to describe the art more closely, it might be called the art of being self-recollected. For it is the collection—or re-collection—of the scattered fragments of the self, immersed in the ten thousand things of the world, into the brilliant, all-embracing light of the Self in the glory of its Oneness.

In presenting this compilation of articles devoted to the subject of meditation, our endeavor has been to cast some light upon the processes and disciplines of meditational procedures. Each writer has approached the discussion in his own unique way. In many of the articles, it is pointed out that meditation involves the totality of an individual's life and activities. A number of writers have suggested specific steps along the way of meditation. For some, a goal must be defined; for others, there is no goal, but only the pointing of the mind in a given direction. The arrow of the self is let loose to pierce the Self. But you alone can draw the bow; you alone can loose the arrow. It is hoped that the essays which follow may indicate in some measure the worthwhileness of learning to be the archer.

1.

Meditation Is "A Flow of Soul"

JAMES S. PERKINS

How empty seems our world of a natural awareness of man's immortality. Every horizon seems bur-
dened with human acquisitiveness and endless concern over the ills and hazards of mortal life. This
view itself is an invitation to meditation. Who has
not felt pressed at times by the turmoil of events, or
the inanity of his material environment, to seek
fresh resources of vitality within himself, awakening
consciousness, if possible, in regions where life is
ever ascendant in undiminishing splendor? If meditation offers such a promise one is reckless to over-
look its possibilities. So much has been written and
said about the subject that the usual approaches to
meditation are commonly known. Yet each individual finds that his own needs and qualities of inner
life incline him in a particular direction, consequently there is always room for another procedure. The
following is

A Theosophical Approach

The simplest idea to be had about meditation is
that it opens the way for *Soul-action*. Since the term
"soul" may be objected to because of its connotations
and vagueness of definition, our first step is to clarify what is meant by the word soul.

Theosophy is especially helpful with its definite

delineation, in experiential terms, of the domains of consciousness that compose man's immortal selfhood. Specifically, the three regions are: *Manas,* which reflects the Universal Mind; *Buddhi,* the all-inclusive energy of pure love; and *Atma,* where the deep center of the Self is radiant with the mystery and power of life's creative source. Accordingly, man's Soul is a triune composite of elements located in these levels of consciousness—a unit that is ever resplendent with its divine nature and potentials. All of the three levels are fields for exploration through procedures of meditation, and in each can be induced little known faculties for self-discovery, and facilities that enable one to open greater orbits of being. Certainly everyone can reach the profound assurance that he is indeed the creator—not merely the creature—of his environment; which spells the difference between being alive only in worldly attachments, with their storms of pleasure-pain-delusion, and being meaningfully and purposefully aware in the Self that never dies.

Meditation for the Theosophist, then, becomes a method that accomplishes a polar reversal—or reorientation—of one's consciousness from its age-old anchorage in matter, subject to the awesome suction into black depths, to that primordial pole-star, one's spiritual center in life's very Source.

Unique Relevance

The more clearly the method used is based upon universal principles and that knowledge "knowing which, all else can be known," the more certainly meditation becomes a spiritual science. But it is a new kind of science that is characterized by its *unique relevance* rather than by its repeatable sameness. While the same vistas and forces are opened by individual explorers, each does so from his own position in time and space, and with results that are unique. The factor of uniqueness upholds—rather than discredits—the validity of individual discoveries. In this light meditation appears to be more an art than a science. And as with artists, each seeker sets forth on his own responsibility to discover reality and Truth, and through endless defeats and triumphs, to open a channel for his "flow of soul."

As for required knowledge, matters are greatly simplified when, through theosophical studies, we arrive at a summary grasp of man's seven principles and the fundamental division of consciousness that occurs in the mental levels. The dividing line is located where matter that responds by producing forms, becomes non-form-producing matter. The student is then able to understand the essential position of incarnated man: that of normal confinement in the transient complex of consciousness composed of a mental, an astral, and a physical vesture; and his necessity to become fully aware in his awakening soul, or immortal upper triad of consciousness, the Manas-Buddhi-Atma assemblage.

What must be sought is an alignment or rapport of both body and soul with the yet deeper center of Self in its own profound levels of imperishable spirit. Effective meditation is designed to meet this need. It becomes a creative performance involving the whole known self. Just as in a ballet dance, the movement of consciousness becomes precise and ordered, following a natural geometry of motion that governs in each of its fields. Space-limitation does not permit an elaboration here of these movements, but the subject has been explained and illustrated in the latter part of my little book *A Geometry of Space and Consciousness.* *

No art or technology becomes such without a

*Theosophical Publishing House, Madras, India, 1964.

period of special preparation. This applies equally to meditation. The structure of one's daily habits becomes required study, and offers also a field of training. Destructive habits are breeders of delusion and doubt that so easily deflect the tentative seekers. There is an occult saying that "the treasure (of enlightenment) is guarded by faithful gnomes and demons." These elementals are within ourselves, ever ready to turn us back into the confinement of our mortal state. If we are serious about meditation, we are actually proposing to bridge the gulf between our visible mundane existence, and the invisible, intangible mystery of the Soul. Normally, one hardly recognizes the Soul's reality; but we intend now to establish far more than a mere nodding acquaintance with it. Cleanliness of life, purity of the mind, and a certain harmlessness of the heart are valuable companions along the way. In fact they accompany us as a mounted guard, so to speak, in the crowded lanes of inner space that are often anything but benign.

If meditation is to become a flow of soul, the flow will be through all three of the mortal vehicles: mental, astral, and physical. These are to be vivified, refined and harmonized, thus rendering each one aligned with the deep spiritual center of the Self through resonances attuned to it. This harmony releases in the vehicles latent energies that will assist us in the hard task of controlling and ordering our states of consciousness.

The Physical Channel

Turning now to performance, creative suggestions are preferable to offering set patterns on "how to meditate." It is important to encourage the individual's awakening to his own method of growth. Of immediate practical value is the hint to regard carefully the automatisms of the several vehicles. We want to make use of their forces by establishing functional routines. Such as, for example, sitting in a comfortable arrangement of the physical body, managing an unharried atmosphere in which to attain quietness of mind and harmony of emotions. Employment may be made of music, incense or any assistance that is available that will aid in bringing full concentration to the task ahead. Clarity as to what we intend to do is a basic need. For as each vehicle is brought into a harmonized state, attention must move onward ahead of any torpor or distraction that might result from physical discomfort, astral fantasies, or mind-wandering tendencies that may readily overtake and defeat us. Our course must rise steadfastly into that higher orbit of being, the Soul, redolent with its own fresh energies to draw upon. This will not happen if we have not, first of all, rendered the physical body, with its usual distresses and impulses, quietly nondisturbing. As we succeed in doing this, we must know what comes next, and to go on, or we will certainly "go to sleep."

There are two facilities available to everyone that can be successfully utilized in moving onward. They are the *breath,* and the *Inner Light.* Breathing can be a primary energizer of the bodies, especially if we conceive the universe to be a shoreless ocean of light and energy that is inexhaustible in subtler levels of consciousness where we, too, have our roots. As we breathe deeply, with full concentration upon the breath being drawn from the sea of Universal Light, down through the mental, astral, and physical bodies, we can visualize it as some clean shower of inbreathed potencies that radiate throughout the whole physical body, harmonizing it. Then, with the outbreathing, we can further render the physical body perfectly still. This effort will be found to have a beneficial effect in quieting the nerves and removing attention from disturbing stresses and discomforts.

Regard well the idea of the *Inner Light,* for we may have failed to note the fact that it is manipulable by the will in man. The first manifestation in universal creation is light, and light is the last energy to withdraw. In our solar universe light radiates at seven velocities or energy levels. There are seven suns in the solar system, one within the other, according to H. P. Blavatsky in *The Secret Doctrine.* The light of the physical sun is the feeblest, hardly extending to the outer reaches of the solar system. We can imagine what, at subtlest levels, must be the quality of light that fills the whole solar universe, where all creatures are children of the sun. The energy that is in the universal light is known by the Sanskrit term *Prana,* which means "breath of life." When we are using the breath as suggested above, we are breathing Prana from higher regions. We can visualize it as the light breathed into, and radiating from that physical center, which can be pictured as a miniature sun within one's own bodily universe.

With the foregoing effort it is possible to realize our whole physical body as light itself, which, in the final atomic analysis it actually is. In its archetypal perfection, the physical body is one of nature's most beautiful forms. Rather than thinking of its repellent features, and of abandoning it in order to reach higher consciousness, an objective can be to expose the body to the light of its archetypal perfection that actually exists in the deep center of our being. As we do so, we will be acting in harmony with nature's gradual transformation of all physical forms as evolution proceeds. The physical body is to be loved and treated with respect, its physical elemental cooperated with intelligently. With this kind of *natural* release from physical demands, our attention can be concentrated elsewhere.

The Astral Channel

Each one's astral situation is unique with its own deeply grooved automatisms of biases, anxieties, wants, dislikes, fears and so on. These must be objectively studied with the intention to establish a self-determined rhythm in the body, at least during the periods of meditation. This can be done by once more using the light with the breath, to clear the astral vehicle of undesirable rhythms and unwanted feelings. With full attention one experiences vividly the qualities determined upon for harmonizing one's astral situation. These may be, for example, qualities of pure love, unattached joy, serene peace and compassion. Each in turn can be experienced by some self-devised means.

The Mental Channel

The next stage of meditation is more difficult, for we must now control the mind with the mind. The prospect would be even more dismaying were we able to see with opened eyes the swiftly coiling currents of light and flashing color that, with every thought, are constantly assuming shapes and projecting influences into the surrounding mental world. These energies, in turn, are attracting to us forms and influences of a similar quality. Can the mind possibly be stilled? Here again, we may begin by studying our mental habits and automatisms. Usually we depend on "the without" for mental stimulation. Consciousness in the mental body seems to be as some creature in the ocean that normally ruminates near the surface of its sphere, searching amidst the rain of impacts for more exciting and interesting material with which to preoccupy itself. This age-old habit of life is overcome by those who discipline and train their minds in specialized fields of activity.

We propose now an even more refined and simpler discipline: that of first emptying the mind completely, then of focusing concentrated attention upon ideas and subtle influences that are arriving from beyond the mundane mind, although seeming to well up from within it. The two mental realms are easily distinguishable by observing the principle that characterizes each. The lower mind is ever turned in upon itself; nothing has relevance but that which serves one's personal interests. The higher mind, on the other hand, is ever turned outward, toward universal horizons, attracted to Truth and Beauty, to eternal principles and lawful structure. The lower mind is confined to its mortal encirclement; the higher mind is free to range the universe. We can now proceed with the task of emptying the mind by using the inbreathing of Prana to sweep the lower mental body clear of all thought forms—breathing them away, and momentarily experiencing a stillness of the mind. It does not matter if the thought forms immediately return, and we find ourselves again "thinking." We can repeat the process. Since the lower mind can entertain only one subject at a time, and we have it now occupied with the emptying procedure, compulsive thinking is halted, and a wonderful quietude can result: our first awareness of true inner peace.

Our meditation has now rendered the physical body radiant with the inner light and perfectly composed; the astral body harmonized and rhythmic; and the mental body energized by emptying it, and rendering it—as some giant mirror—reflective of subtle influences from the higher mind. We have thus created out of the lower self a tool of consciousness for contacting the Soul's fields of knowledge and Truth. With continued refinement the tool becomes an instrument of direct illumination and conveyor of knowledge from the Teacher within one's Self.

We might pause at this point to gather the fruits of meditation, to contemplate exalted concepts and noble utterances that appeal to us, realizing profoundly their application in our lives. Perhaps it would be well not to venture into further stages of meditation until we have gained more experience and confidence in this new instrument. There is so much to be learned and so little known of the potentials that are latent in our natures. Later, as we feel it desirable to do so, we can proceed with more advanced explorations.

The Dual Mind

When we do undertake further ventures, we are confronted at once with the dual character of the mind. Theosophy is specific about the division that exists in the mental levels between the three higher subdivisions of non-form-making material, and the four lower levels in which forms are automatically created with every impulse of thought that takes place in the concrete mind. The two parts are of an entirely different character, yet are so merged with one another, that they have been likened to the silver in mother-of-pearl. Our task is that of becoming focused in the silver while ignoring the mother-of-pearl. Here, we may appreciate the information available regarding a passageway that links the lower with the higher mind, namely, the *Antahkarana*. Without entering into the mysteries of its nature (a subject that should be given careful study) we will simply refer to it in passing, noting that when we are in meditation and the lower mind is rendered reflective of the higher, the reflections occur via the Antahkarana. And even more significant is the fact that consciousness crosses this bridge of Antahkarana when it passes from its focus in the mental body to its higher center in Manas, the immortal mind. People unconsciously make this transit into the higher fields of Manas whenever their thinking is abstract, profound, or inspired. There is no need for them to be aware of the bridge they cross. However, a knowledge of this facility will assist the meditator to move with clearer awareness and purpose toward conscious entry, at will, into the regions of the Soul. The transition occurs temporarily in meditation. But as the whole nature becomes repolarized, consciousness will remain permanently centered in the higher Self.

This brings up the question: How does one deliberately elevate consciousness from the lower to the higher mind? Each individual has his own natural way of doing this, such as listening to music, the reading of poetry or scriptural passages, or by observing beauty in nature. However, in meditation we have selected a time and place to accomplish this transition with no aids other than those of our inner resources. The principle to be used by everyone is demonstrable in anyone by his sounding with utmost intensity some note of greatness, within himself, that activates the higher Manas. This is, of course, an individual matter. If you are a creative artist, for example, the method used might be a vividly visualized creation of some heroic masterpiece of painting. Its swift realization charges one with a measure of the power and love that really would be present in such an experience. Then by becoming absorbed in the structural design, imaged as underlying the painted form, he can open the play of will in the geometry of forces that uphold the structural form. This makes possible his permitting the divine geometry to thrust consciousness onward into realms of Universal Law and Truth. Consciousness follows a natural path to the heights.

Such an exercise, for some temperaments, will span not only the whole realm of Manas, but reach and enter the domains of Buddhi, even touching levels that reflect the Atmic Selfhood. Any of the arts can be utilized. Or, one can turn to mantras, spiritual ceremonies and heroic or sacrificial acts—all of which voice the languages of the Soul. To generate force in this way, yet not turn a single physical hair in the effort, results in an immense release of inner energy. This is the Soul-energy that is indispensable for moving onward self-reliantly into deeper realms of Truth. Strangely, the same energy release is obtainable by facing up to personal disasters, to human extremities of pain, sorrow, fear, and loneliness. By "dying" in these experiences—which is to say, by penetrating with perfect integrity their "inevitable worst"—one can open the way through darkness into the Light beyond. But whatever the method adopted, if it is effective, a truly miraculous occurrence takes place. For there has been a crossing over of the giant chasm of *Avidya,* of "not-knowing," that separates man, the mortal—trapped as he is, in his materialized form—from the immortal true Man, experienced heretofore only as reflected through art, heroic action, and self-less love. This formidable chasm will have been crossed on the silvery bridge of Antahkarana, the gates of which can now be closed against the marauding forages of the lower self with its elemental hungers, its atavistic and violent disturbances. On one side of the silvery gates, composed of nonattachment, there is nothing but death and transition; on the other is self-awareness in immortality. Here, a peace is known that is not found in the worlds of strife.

We will now find for ourselves that concentrated intellectual attention focused in Manas is only reflective of Buddhi; consciousness does not thereby move into Buddhi. Although we may go with the mind to the Buddhic realm, we do not move about in it with the mind. One can *think* all day long about love, but there is no experience of love unless one does love. So, we enter Buddhi by means of another loco-motion of consciousness—that of selfless Universal Love, which ever flows outward away from the Self. One has actually to experience this love-identity with all things if one is to explore with Buddhic conscious-ness. It is accomplished by becoming "at-one"—identified with—what is being contemplated. This is the way of knowing truly the lives around us from within, by becoming united with them, rather than separated from them through mental appraisal, com-parison, and classification. The heart alone is con-cerned in this knowing by being. It is with the Buddhic consciousness that the element of compas-sionate altruism associated with Universal Brother-hood is experienced and understood. Anyone who feels an out-pouring of glad thanksgiving when he glimpses some incident of the Good, the True, and the Beautiful is receiving thereby pulsations from his Buddhic realms of consciousness. All experiences of it are jewelled moments, of which we have so few in a lifetime. These are the gems that one must cultivate, and collect, and use in meditation.

If our exploration continues, it will be through awakening consciousness in the Atmic level of the Soul. Atma is characterized chiefly by the universal lawfulness that reflects perfectly the Cosmic Will in creation. This brings into view horizons of Truth that are strictly for individual exploration and utter-ance. And it is at this point that one may perceive the full majesty and scope of the freedom that is cham-pioned by The Theosophical Society. Consciousness moving upward through Buddhic universal love, ar-rives in Atma as awareness of the pristine purpose of the Immortal Soul. This sense of spiritual purpose is wonderfully expressed in the Sanskrit term *dharma,* in Indian thought. Great Adepts have explored the Nirvanic regions of Atma, and left invaluable records of its nature. The student-explorer can now appreciate the rich heritage of wisdom that has been transmitted.

With an opening of this highest level of the Immortal Self, we have begun to align consciousness with the center, around which can take place a polar reorientation of our lives. The all-important alignment of the Soul's consciousness in Atma-Buddhi-Manas with its mortal unit of mental, astral, and physical vehicles, takes place first in meditation. Then gradually a reorientation is experienced that changes the great tidal currents of our lives, and they are increasingly graced by the pure "flow of Soul."

We need not expect supernormal powers, perfect wisdom, and ultimate bliss as a result, but if we have used intelligently the knowledge available, we will open clearer, deeper insights into Truth; we will know an unshakable sense of direction; and more wondrous than all, we will begin to experience a continuous flow of teaching, as "day unto day uttereth speech, and night unto night revealeth knowledge."

Meditation will have become for us a way of swift timeless movement into an immense association with Space and Reality, and a constant awareness of the imperishable Real within the perishing forms—the Immortal Self seated serenely in control of its realigned mortal vestures.

2.

The Significance of Meditation in Buddhism

LAMA ANAGARIKA GOVINDA

The precondition of every religious practice or meditation is the recognition of divine or eternal qualities in man, qualities whose awakening or realization constitutes the aim of religious life. If we do not believe in a supreme, all-transcending value, inherent in man and attainable by him, then the very reason and starting point for any kind of spiritual aspiration is missing. That is why the Buddha proclaimed faith as the first prerequisite of the spiritual way:

> *Aparuta tesam amatassa dvara,*
> *ye sotavanto, pamuncantu saddham!*
> Wide open are the gates of immortality,
> Ye that have ears to hear, release your faith!

However, the faith *(saddha)* which the Buddha demanded was not the blind faith in dogmas, revelations, gods, or human authorities (including his own), but the faith in ourselves, in our own higher nature, and the possibility to realize it, to attain liberation.

"Liberation" can have a meaning only if there is something that can be liberated, and this "something" can be nothing other than the living power, the manifestation of universal forces that create and maintain the individual streams of consciousness. The very fact that Buddhism believes in the continuity of karmically conditioned, self-perpetuating conscious forces, moving through endless cycles of reincarnations, proves that it recognizes an indestructible power or quality, which is maintained through countless lives and deaths.

The question which arises from this is not how to destroy that power, but how to lift it from the narrow tracks of a never-ending ever-reptitive cycle into the freedom and all-pervasiveness of an enlightened consciousness. Due to habit, which is a form of inertia caused by "ego-sclerosis," i.e. by the calcification or hardening of our egohood at a certain stage of our individual development, man is in danger of cutting himself off from his universal heritage and contenting himself with the lesser, though the greatest of all values is available to him. It is the greatest good that the Buddha is concerned with. That he not only believed in it, but actually attained and realized it himself, is proved by the fact of his Enlightenment.

On this the whole edifice of Buddhism is based. For the individual it is the highest aim; for the teaching, however, it is the starting-point. The teaching, therefore, is rightly called "Buddhism," the doctrine of Enlightenment. It is the idea of Enlightenment and not that of suffering (as so many Western critics of Buddhism believe) which gives Buddhism its character. Just as medicine is first and foremost the science of healing (and the Buddha, indeed, has been called "the great Healer" or *"Bhaisajyaguru,"* the Supreme Physician) but not the science of disease— though the knowledge of disease is necessary for the knowledge of healing. For the same reason the Buddha had to understand first the nature of suffering, in order to be able to show the way toward its overcoming, the way to happiness. However, the idea of suffering and its annihilation on the path of morality, renunciation, and knowledge, is common to all religious systems of India.

What was new in the Buddha's doctrine was that he recognized individuality as a flowing, ever-changing, self-transforming living force, evolving or developing to an inner law, in contradistinction to an unchangeable, self-contained, and separate soul-substance, as assumed by primitive animism and popular belief. In this way he raised his doctrine to the level of a dynamic world-view, in which individuality was liberated from the rigor mortis of separateness, and the idea of universality from the negative conception of a "merging into the All," which—if we want to be honest—is only a poetical way of expressing complete dissolution of all faculties of life and consciousness, corresponding to the materialistic notion of last century's science that, at death, the various elements and forces that constituted the individual are indiscriminately dissolved and dispersed into their inorganic constituents. This would degrade the individual to a meaningless accident in the universal scheme, and to assume this would require a point of view that arrogates to the human intellect the role of a superior judge—which again contradicts the very theory of the accidental nature of individuality. Thus we can only arrive at the conclusion that individuality is a necessary, important, and meaningful expression of the universe of its inherent divine consciousness or ultimate reality. Consequently individuality and universality are not mutually exclusive values, but two sides of the same reality, compensating each other and becoming one in the experience of Enlightenment.

In this experience it is not the mind that dissolves into an amorphous All, but it is the realization that the individual itself contains the totality of the universe focalized in its very core. Thus, it is the world that hitherto was experienced as an external reality, that merges or is integrated into the enlightened mind in the moment in which the universality of consciousness is realized. This is the ultimate moment of the liberation from the impediments and fetters of ignorance and illusion.

We are still captured by crude similies of quantitative magnitudes in place of qualitative values, when we compare the ultimate experience of liberation with the "drop that slips into the shining sea." It would be more appropriate—though paradoxical from the point of view of three-dimensional logic—to say that the "sea slips into the shining drop." Because the drop is qualitatively not different from the sea. All the oceans that cover the earth, as seen from the distance of the sun, are not more than a drop in the immensity of space; and a drop, as seen from the standpoint of a microorganism contained in it, is as vast as an ocean.

It is not the extension of the mind that matters (or the expansion of consciousness), but its intensity, which makes it into a radiating "incandescent" center of the universe, a center in which the universe becomes conscious of itself. And this alone is the ultimate aim and purpose of meditation. The demonstration of the universality of man and of his capacity of attaining self-realization in the supreme experience of Enlightenment—without the intervention of gods, priests, dogmas, and sacrificial rituals—on the direct way of meditation: this is what the Buddha gave to the world, and which has become the very core of Buddhism, irrespective of differences created by sects, philosophical schools, or scholastic traditions or by racial or linguistic influences.

Meditation, however, does not concern only the mind, but the whole human being, including his bodily functions and activities. Therefore the first step toward meditation consists in taking stock of the situation in which we find ourselves. Meditation means many things: it means turning inward; it means quiet observation, reflection, and awareness of ourselves and the world around us; it means to be conscious of consciousness, to become a detached observer of the stream of changing thoughts, feelings, drives, and visions, until we recognize their nature and their origin.

But these are only the first steps of meditation, while in the more advanced stages we change from the role of a more or less intellectual observer to that of an experiencer of a deeper reality, namely of the timeless and universal source of all the phenomena we observe in the contemplation of our stream of consciousness and even in the simplest bodily functions, as for instance in the process of breathing, which in itself can be a subject of meditation, because it reveals the very nature of life in its alternate inward and outward movement, in its continual process of receiving and releasing, of taking and of giving back, of the deep relationship between the inner and the outer world, the individual and the universe.

However, between and beyond the two alternative movements, so to say at the turning point between them, there is a moment of stillness, in which the inner and the outer world coincide and become one, since there is nothing that can be called either "inside" or "outside." This moment, in which time stands still, because it is empty of all designations of time, space and movement, but which nevertheless is a moment of infinite potentialities, represents the state of pure "being" or "is-ness," expressed by the word *sunyata*, the all-containing void or metaphysical emptiness, beyond definition, beyond any kind of "thingness" or conceptual limitation, which, therefore, may be called "no-*thing*-ness" or the primordial ground from which everything originates. It is the timeless moment before creation or, seen from the standpoint of the individual, the moment of pure receptivity that precedes all creative activity.

It is the first movement in the great symphonic *mandala,* or magic circle, in which our inner world appears as sound and light, color and form, thought and vision, rhythm and harmonious coordination, visible symbol and meditative experience. This first *movement*—which expression may be taken in the musical as well as in the spiritual and *emotional* sense—corresponds to the first profound meditative attitude or experience, called "The Wisdom of the Great Mirror" or the "Mirror-like Wisdom" *(adarsa-jnana).*

In the light of the Mirror-like Wisdom things are freed from their "thingness," their isolation, without being deprived of their form; they are divested of their materiality (like the reflections in a mirror, which can neither be said to be inside or outside of the mirror) without being dissolved, because the creative principle of the mind, which is at the bottom of all form and materiality, is recognized as the active side of the Universal Consciousness *(alaya-vijnana)* on the surface of which forms arise and pass away, like the waves on the surface of the ocean, which latter, when stilled, reflects the pure emptiness of space and the pure light of heaven (the two aspects of *sunyata)* .

Hui-Neng, the Sixth Patriarch of the Ch'an School, once said: "When you hear me speak about the void, do not fall into the idea that I mean vacuity. The illimitable void of the universe is capable of holding myriads of things of various shapes and forms, such as the sun and the moon, and the stars, worlds . . . heavenly planes and hells, great oceans and all the mountains . . . . Space takes in all these, and so does the voidness of our nature. We say that Essence of Mind is great, because it embraces all things, since all things are within our nature."

If *sunyata* hints at the nonsubstantiality of the world and the interrelationship of all beings and things, then there can be no better word to describe its meaning than *transparency*. This word avoids the pitfalls of a pure negation and replaces the concepts of substance, resistance, impenetrability, limitation, materiality, by something that can be positively experienced and is closely related to the concepts of space and light. The transparency of the mind-created body, the *vajra-kaya* or "Diamond Body," visualized in tantric meditation, symbolizes *sunyata* in visible form, thus bearing out the above-mentioned interpretation. Here "form" is no more in opposition to space, but form and space penetrate each other in a luminous and dynamic play of light and color. The conception of *jiji-mu-ge* (Japanese; lit., "each thing no hindrance") has its origin in this interaction of form and emptiness, or form and space, which is experienced in the realization of the ultimate transparency of the world: the world as a phenomenon of consciousness. Without consciousness there is neither form nor its concomitant notion of emptiness. Consciousness determines the world in which we live or the particular aspect under which the universe appears to us; in itself it is neither this nor that, it is *sunyata*.

Thus the Mirror-like Wisdom reflects with the impartiality of a mirror the nature of all things and of ourselves, while remaining unaffected and untouched by the image it reflects. It is the attitude of the impartial observer, the pure, spontaneous awareness, which in Zen Buddhism is called *satori* or *kensho*: "seeing into one's own nature."

By recognizing our own nature as *sunyata,* we realize that it is not different from the essential nature of all living beings; and herefrom arises the "second movement" of meditation, in which we realize the oneness of all life, the solidarity of all sentient beings. This is the "Equalizing Wisdom" or the "Wisdom of Equality *(sumata-jnana)*, in which we turn from the cool and detached attitude of an observer to the warm human feeling of all-embracing love and compassion for all that lives. Already in the *Dhammapada* (Pali) this essential equality with others has been made the keystone of Buddhist ethics, when it was said that "having made oneself equal to others" or "recognizing oneself in others" one should abstain from hurting others, which shows that compassion in Buddhism is not based on moral or mental superiority, but on the feeling of oneness.

If, however, this feeling remains confined to the merely emotional plane, it may lead to a purely sentimental and one-sided attitude, in which the feeling of oneness deprives the individual of responsibility, action, and discrimination in a world that is not merely a featureless unity but an organic whole in which differentiation is as much an expression of reality as of oneness, and form is as important as emptiness, since both depend on each other, condition each other like light and shade.

Thus we come to the "third movement" of meditative experience, in which we are concerned neither with concrete beings nor with material things, but where both differentiation and unity, form and emptiness, the purity of light and the infinite modulations of color, are revealed in their infinite interrelatedness without losing their distinctive qualities and individuality of expression. This is the "Distinguishing Wisdom" *(pratyaveksana-jnana)* in which our mundane mind, our discriminating, judging intellect turns into the intuitive consciousness of inner vision, in which the "special and general characteristics of all things become clearly visible without hindrances (*asanga;* i.e., spontaneously) and in which the unfoldment of various spiritual faculties takes place."

Through this wisdom the functions of the group of discriminating processes, which we sum up under the general term of perception (*samjna-skandha*) are turned inward and become transformed and intensified into creative transcendental vision (*dhyana*), in which the individual characteristics of all phenomena and their general and universal relations become apparent. This wisdom is represented by Buddha Amitabha, the Buddha of Infinite Light, who is shown in the gesture of meditation (*dhyana-mudra*).

The "fourth movement" of meditative experience belongs to the realm of action and will power and represents the "All-Accomplishing Wisdom" or "the Wisdom that Accomplishes All Works." Here volition (*samskara-skandha*) is transformed into selfless, "karma-free" action of a life dedicated to the realization of Enlightenment, motivated by compassion and based on the understanding of both the individual and the universal aspects of life and phenomena, as experienced in the previous three movements. In the Vijnaptimatra-Siddhi-Shastra it has been said that "this kind of consciousness manifests itself for the benefit of all living beings . . . in the three kinds of transformed actions . . ." namely those of body, speech, and mind, "according to the vow," namely that of the Bodhisattva, whose "body" is the universe (*dharma-kaya*), whose "speech" is the mantric word, the word of truth and power, and whose "mind" is the universal consciousness.

Each of these four movements is represented by a gesture (*mudra*) of the respective four transcendental

Buddhas who symbolize these states of meditative consciousness and experience, and occupy the successive places in the *mandala*, beginning with the east and moving via south and west to the north. The position in the *mandala*, therefore, indicates not only a spatial position in the visible diagram but also a sequence in time, i.e., in the unfoldment or process of meditation.

Thus the Buddha of the eastern quarter of the *mandala*, *Aksobhya*, the Immutable One, who embodies the pure inward-directed awareness of the basic mirror-like consciousness, points with his right hand toward the earth (representing the totality of the past which the Buddha called up as a witness before his Enlightenment) with the palm *inward*, while the passive left hand—as in the case of all the four Dhyani-Buddhas, representing the Four Wisdoms—rests in the lap with the palm upward.

The Buddha of the southern quarter of the *mandala*, *Ratnasambhava*, the Jewel-Born, who embodies the Wisdom of Equality, expresses the feeling of solidarity and love toward all living beings by the gesture of giving, similar to the previous one, but with the palm turned *outward*.

The Buddha of the western quarter of the *mandala*, *Amitabha*, the Buddha of Infinite Light, who embodies the Wisdom of Distinguishing Inner Vision, is represented in the gesture of meditation: both hands with palms upward, resting upon each other in the lap.

The Buddha of the northern quarter of the *mandala*, *Amoghasiddhi*, the Realizer of the Aim, who embodies the Wisdom that Accomplishes All Works, i.e. of selfless action, is represented in the gesture of fearlessness, expressing at the same time reassurance and blessing. His right hand is raised to the height of the shoulder and the palm is turned *outward* in the gesture of blessing the world.

It may be noticed that in each of these cases the palm of the active right hand follows the direction of consciousness. And in this connection it might be mentioned that the upturned palms in the gesture of meditation (*dhyana-mudra*) signify a receptivity toward the eternal qualities and forces of the universe. The palms are like open bowls, ready to receive the gifts of heaven.

The passive left hand of all these Buddhas is always shown in this attitude, because our essential, though unconscious, relationship to the universe is common to all stages of meditation. Besides the direction of the palms we have to consider the three planes or levels of these gestures. The first two are on the basic level and point toward the earth; the *dhyana-mudra* is on the middle level, which represents "Man," in whom "Heaven" and "Earth" are united; the fourth gesture is on the universal level, where wisdom turns into spiritual action. On this level we also find the fifth gesture, which belongs to the central Buddha of the *mandala, Vairocana,* the Radiating One, who represents the sum total of the Four Wisdoms, namely the Universal Law. His gesture is the "setting in motion the Wheel of the Law" (*dharmacakra-mudra*). In this gesture both hands are active on the level of the heart center: the left hand turned inward, the right turned outward. Thus the inner and the outer world are united in the ultimate realization, as well as in the primordial state of universality.

The position of these Dhyani-Buddhas or their symbols—be it in form of *mudras,* colors, mantras, or emblems (like wheel, vajra, jewel, lotus, mirror, etc.)—does not only indicate a spatial position in the *mandala,* but a sequence in time, a development of unfoldment of spiritual qualities in the process of meditation, which comprises the totality of human consciousness and all its faculties, such as awareness, feeling, perception, volition, and all mental activities.

The *mandala* is like a map of the inner world which we want to explore and realize in the great venture of meditation. Without such a map and the capacity to read it, i.e. without the knowledge of its symbolism, we are like travelers who set out on a journey without any conception of route or direction. It is for this reason that the study of psychology was of such importance to the followers of the Buddha from the earliest times, as the systematic representations of the *Abidharma* (as in the Pali *Abhidhammattha-Sangaha* or the Sanskrit *Abhidharma-Kosha*) show, out of which the later Tantric *sadhanas* with their meticulous psychological details and *mandalas* grew.

"The aim of all the Tantras," as Guiseppe Tucci, one of the great explorers of Tantric Buddhism, says, "is to teach the ways whereby we may set free the divine light which is mysteriously present and shining in each of us, although it is enveloped in an insidious web of the psyche's weaving." In this aim all Buddhist systems of meditation are united, though their ways may differ, but as long as they recognize the Four Wisdoms as the basis of all meditative practices, they shall never lose that spiritual balance on which the final success of them all depends. That this was recognized not only in the general Mahayana literature and in Indian and Tibetan Tantras, but equally in Chinese Ch'an and Japanese Zen, becomes evident from Rinsai's (Lin-chi was his Chinese name) "Fourfold Contemplation."* Explaining his meditational method Rinsai made the following statement:

> At the first instance I destroy the Man and not the object.

---

*Katto-Shu, part II, leaf No. 27B-28a; cfr. Ohasama-Faust "Zen der lebendige Buddhismus in Japan," Perthes, Gotha-Stuttgart, 1925.

> At the second instance I destroy the object but
> not the Man.
> At the third instance I destroy both: the Man
> and the object.
> At the fourth instance I destroy none of them:
> neither the man nor the object.

This statement, which on the surface sounds like a
paradoxical Zen *koan,* is in reality a sober assessment
of the subject-object relationship in the experience of
the Four Wisdoms.

In the Mirror-like Wisdom the pure *objective*
awareness prevails while the notion of the subject
(Man) is absent.

In the Wisdom of the Essential Equality of all bē-
ings, the subject (Man) becomes the only conscious
reality without an object.

In the Wisdom of Distinguishing Vision both subject and object lose their independent reality and are
seen in their mutually dependent relationship on the
universal stage in their eternal interplay of emptiness
and form, in which materiality, thingness, and the
illusion of separate entities give way to the transparency of creative vision. It was this experience, according to the Buddha's own words, that characterized
his Enlightenment.

In the All-accomplishing Wisdom of selfless action,
subject and object are restored to their functional
status of polarity on the plane of the three-dimensional world of existential—i.e. relative—reality. Thus,
"neither the Man nor the object" is destroyed, and
we have returned into our familiar world, where
"mountains are again mountains and waters are again
waters" (to use the well-known Zen phrase), but
where we see them with new eyes that are no more
veiled by the illusion of egoity and separateness, freed
from craving and possessiveness as well as from
enmity and aversion. *Samsara* has turned into *Nir-*

vana, the mundane world has turned into a gigantic *mandala,* in which every form has become an expression of total reality and every living being a unique manifestation of a greater life and a universal consciousness in which we all share.

Thus the meditative experience of the Four Wisdoms has revealed itself as a tremendous symphony of four movements, in which the pendulum of experience swings from passive awareness to active emotion, from creative vision to selfless action, comprising all faculties of mind and feeling, imagination and observation, oneness and differentiation, sense-perception and intuition. It results in the transformation of *all* faculties of man, until he has become *complete.*

This completeness cannot be achieved through negations—for which reason the Buddha rejected asceticism—nor through the one-sided affirmation of the one or the other of our basic faculties. Feeling has to be balanced by knowledge, intuition has to be balanced by clear thought, contemplation has to be balanced by action. Those who believe that by mere passive sitting they can attain enlightenment are as far from the mark as those who believe that they can achieve liberation by mere learnedness or pious recitation of sacred texts. This was pointed out already by the ancient Ch'an Master Tai-hui when he wrote to his disciple Chen-ju Tao-jen: "There are two forms of error now prevailing among followers of Zen, laymen as well as monks. The one thinks that there are wonderful things hidden in words and phrases, and those who hold this view try to learn many words and phrases. The second goes to the other extreme forgetting that words are the pointing finger, showing one where to locate the moon. Blindly following the instruction given in the sutras, where words are said to hinder the right understanding of the truth of Zen and Buddhism, they reject all verbal teachings and simply sit with eyes closed, letting down the eyebrows as if they were completely dead. Only when these two erroneous views are done away with, is there a chance for real advancement of Zen."*

This sound advice is as true nowadays as it was then and applies not only to Zen but to all methods of meditation.

*Translated from the German version, quoted by Ohasama-Faust in *Zen, der lebendige Buddhismus in Japan.*

3.

Some Interesting Aspects of Meditation

I. K. TAIMNI

The word "meditation" stands for a large variety of mental exercises adopted by people who have a spiritual ideal of one kind or another in their lives and want to realize this ideal at least to some extent. As the mental activity and discipline involved in meditation is of very wide scope it is not easy to deal here with the subject systematically and comprehensively. Those who read this article are expected to be familiar with the general aspects of meditation. We shall therefore confine ourselves to the discussion of a few interesting aspects of meditation which are not generally understood but are of vital interest to those who are serious about the problems of inner life and do not want to go through their meditation as a mere routine.

It is also not easy to define the purpose of meditation as this depends upon the mental background, temperament, and spiritual evolution of the individual. But it may be indicated in most general terms by saying that this purpose is to bring the lower personality in conscious touch with the Higher Self, thus making it increasingly aware of its divine origin, destiny, and nature. All those people who meditate regularly as part of a systematic spiritual discipline must believe that behind the physical world is hidden a real spiritual world of unimaginable splendor and it is possible for a human being to come in contact with this inner world in an increasing measure by means of meditation. Otherwise, there would be no point in engaging in this kind of mental activity.

The world of Reality is hidden within the mind of every human being and can be known more and more fully by penetrating progressively into deeper levels of the mind. This is why it is necessary in every true spiritual discipline not only to deal with the mind in various ways but also to go into its deeper levels through meditation.

Ordinary knowledge can be acquired through mental activity which is confined to what may be called the surface of things, to the observation of physical phenomena, the collection of sensory data and, working upon this data, through the mental processes of comparison, reasoning, etc. But knowledge concerning the invisible subtler worlds of a mental nature hidden within the physical world cannot be acquired in this manner. It is necessary to go into the deeper levels of mind and consciousness by means of well-defined techniques which are part of yogic discipline.

The difference between these two kinds of mental activity can be understood by comparison with the technique of swimming. An individual who has learnt to swim on the surface of water can explore everything which is present on the surface. The whole world in contact with the surface of the oceans is open to him for observation and investigation. But many worlds of infinite variety lie hidden beneath the surface of the ocean at various depths and in various localities and he can come in contact with these worlds and investigate them only when he learns to dive, to go beneath the surface into the deeper levels of the water. The process of diving is somewhat different from that of ordinary swimming on the surface and involves problems and techniques of a different kind. The difference between ordinary mental activity and meditation is of a similar nature.

Ordinary thinking, even when it is deep and purposeful, involves only movements of the mind on the surface. In rigorous reasoning, which represents perhaps the highest and most difficult form of this kind of mental activity, the mind moves in a disciplined manner, but still the movement is superficial, if we may say so. It is not movement in increasing depth of the mind. The mind may be engaged in prolonged and concentrated mental activity, but as long as it moves in this manner it can deal with and know only what is related to our external life. All achievements in the realm of the mind, even those of a remarkable nature, are possible through this kind of mental activity, but the subtler and more real worlds hidden within the deeper levels of the mind cannot be explored and known in this manner. This requires a different kind of mental activity which may be referred to as movement of mind in depth. In this kind of mental activity, also, the mind moves but the individual tries at the same time to penetrate progressively into its deeper levels. What movement of the mind in depth means will be fully understood on studying the *Yoga-Sutras*.

The above idea provides probably a clue to the secret of successful meditation and shows us why, in the case of most people, meditation is not able to achieve its real aim, namely, progressive contact with the deeper levels of the mind owing to increasing penetrating power of perception. The movement of mind in depth which is necessary for successful meditation naturally requires not only a somewhat different kind of movement but also more effort.

Most of us who have learnt to use our mind efficiently don't realize that the exercise of the mind in a particular kind of activity becomes almost effortless after a time; in fact, we cannot be really efficient until it becomes effortless. The experienced speaker can go on speaking fluently once he has mastered the technique of choosing and arranging his ideas, while standing, and expressing them without a break. The ideas are already there in his mind, trivial or profound, perhaps expressed hundreds of times already, and it is only a question of picking and choosing among them and expressing them continuously. The experienced columnist takes up his pen and reels off pages after pages of commentary almost effortlessly. He has only to choose his ideas from the flood of printed matter which is coming out of the press and express them in a striking manner. Once the technique of marshalling ideas and expressing them effectively has been mastered, the rest is easy.

This, it will be seen, is not unlike learning to swim. Once a person has acquired the simple knack of keeping afloat on the water, swimming becomes merely a matter of physical stamina and certain movements of the body. No particular effort, in the real sense, is then needed for continuing to swim.

Most of our mental activities are of this nature. Our mind moves in accustomed grooves or is exercised almost effortlessly in doing things the technique of which has been mastered in an adequate degree. It has not to be kept concentrated or pushing in one direction by an effort of the will or by the overpowering attraction of an object to be accomplished or known. It is therefore not used for sustained mental effort guided by a definite objective and motivated by a continuous pressure of will or attraction—exactly what is needed for successful meditation.

So, merely sitting down in a certain posture and making the mind bring up a connected series of ideas on a chosen subject is not real meditation though this is all that most people do. It will be seen that this kind of mental exercise is really like writing an essay without pen and paper or giving a lecture without speaking. Neither can the common practice of allowing the mind to move in accustomed and well-worn grooves created by repetition of religious texts, be considered as meditation in the true sense, though this is what most religious people do when they "meditate" during their daily religious observance. We tend to cast every kind of necessary activity into a routine so that the mind has not to make much effort and has not to make a choice between alternative courses of action or ideas. This also accounts for the great popularity of rituals in carrying out our religious duties. The idea is to have at least the form of religious life if not its substance. But anyone can see that stagnation is inevitable under these conditions. There is perhaps no greater obstacle on the path of spiritual unfoldment than the false sense of achievement and security engendered by routinism.

Why is it not possible to produce the required mental state when we sit down to meditate? Mainly because our interest in things on which we want to meditate is not adequately intense and deep. We probably imagine that we want to find the reality which we believe is hidden within the deeper layers of our mind and consciousness. But this is a mere vague thought motivated by an equally vague wish. There is no clearly defined and dynamic purpose, no intensity of desire in the background of our mind to solve the problems of our inner life and unravel the mysteries of our existence. To have a qualitative idea of this particular kind of mental state we have to recall the tremendous intensity of purpose and concentration which characterized the mind of a scientist such as Edison when he was working on a scientific invention. His mind was so deeply absorbed in the pursuit of his aim that he forgot even to eat and sleep. That is the kind of mental state which is needed for real meditation and when it is present results appear quickly as pointed out in the *Yoga-Sutras.* (I-21)

This condition is not present because we have not fulfilled certain basic conditions for treading the path of spiritual unfoldment through meditation. We are not really aware of the tremendous illusions and limitations under which we are living our present life and therefore there is no real urge to get out of this condition. The attractions of things down here are too powerful and provide a constant irresistible force for distracting the mind. The mind has not been trained properly to accomplish worthwhile tasks which we have set before ourselves. The ideal does not attract us with sufficient force. In short, we don't possess the essential qualifications.

It is to provide the right conditions for the successful practice of meditation that all true systems of spiritual culture insist on preliminary training of the mind and character. In the well-known *Sadhana-Chatushthaya,* the four-fold system of Self-culture, it is necessary first to acquire the four basic qualifications for treading the Path. These are called in Sanskrit *Viveka, Vairagya, Shattsampatti,* and *Mumuk-shattva.* It is only at a fairly advanced stage of progress that the practice of intensive meditation is taken up to open the channels between the lower and the higher and establish the center of consciousness on the spiritual planes of manifestation.

In treading the path of Raja Yoga outlined in the *Yoga-Sutras,* the aspirant has first to practice *Bahi-ranga* or External Yoga to prepare himself for the practice of meditation with its three stages of *Dharana, Dhyana,* and *Samadhi.* He is not expected to begin even the practice of *Dharana* until he has mas-

tered the fourth technique of *Pranayama,* as is clear
from Sutra II-53.

In every system of Yoga the candidate is expected
to possess the basic qualifications for practicing Yoga
even when this is not specifically mentioned. If he
does not possess them in an adequate degree he is first
made to go through rigorous training for this purpose. It is only in psuedo systems of Yoga that so-
called *Gurus* take on pupils and initiate them into
the mysteries of "transcendental meditation" or
Samadhi without even enquiring whether they possess the necessary qualifications or capacity for this
purpose. To do so would seriously affect their clien-
tele.

Those of us who cannot meditate successfully should
do a little heart-searching and self-introspection. It
will be possible then to see for ourselves that the fundamental cause of this failure is probably lack of serious purpose and earnestness. We start the practice
of meditation before we really want those things
which are the object of meditation. This is like putting the cart before the horse. We must have real
problems before we proceed to solve those problems.
The object of meditation is to solve the problems of
the inner life by penetrating into the deeper layers
of mind and consciousness, where alone the solution
to these problems can be found. If these problems do
not exist for us, there is no use in sitting down to
meditate day after day to solve these problems. Meditation is not an end in itself. It is merely a means to
an end.

I am reminded in this connection of the mentality
of many students who come to the universities for
research. They want to do research, but if you ask
them what problems they want to solve, they have no
answer. You have to give them a problem to work on.
In academic life it is possible to want to do research

first and seek for a problem afterwards because the object of such students is not really research but training for research which will enable them to undertake real research afterwards. But for an aspirant who has to penetrate into the unknown realms of the mind by his own efforts this is obviously impossible. In his case there will be no incentive and therefore no urge for the mind to leave the realm of the known and go within itself to discover what lies hidden within the deeper layers of consciousness.

It is only when the problems are real and the result of our own deep thought and experience, and not problems which we have created artificially or adopted from others, that the intuitive faculty begins to function in meditation and spiritual knowledge which throws light on these problems begins to well up naturally from within.

We should not forget that in using the mind in real meditation we are trying to deal with the realities of life and there should be present not only real problems but a real urge to solve those problems. Intuition can function only in this kind of mental atmosphere of realism and if sincerity and earnestness are not present in an adequate degree the very basic requirements for gaining intuitive knowledge from within are absent and meditation is bound to be barren and frustrating.

When the problems of the inner life become real for us they not only permeate our whole life but their solution becomes a matter of urgency. Even when the lower mind is engaged in external activities the higher mind in the background is constantly brooding over these problems and seeking their solution. This constant brooding over a problem is called *Bhavana* in Sanskrit and is a necessary part of real meditation which brings the intuitive faculty into play. The effect of this constant brooding is further enhanced by *Japa* in which the potency present in "sound" is utilized to reinforce the effect of thought. The student will be able to understand in the light of what has been said above the significance of aphorism I-28 in the *Yoga-Sutras*.

It is necessary to note carefully that all knowledge concerning the spiritual realities of life is gained not through the intellectual faculty of reason but through the little known and much suspected spiritual faculty of intuition. True intuition is not a mysterious but unreliable capacity for guessing truth as is generally supposed by people with an essentially materialistic outlook. It is the faculty of direct perception or awareness of truth which results when the consciousness of the seeker somehow becomes attuned to the Divine Consciousness. In this Consciousness all realities of existence are present externally in their true form, and in the exercise of ordinary intuition in the early stages the consciousness of the seeker leaps, as it were, over the barriers of the intellect and can know any reality at least partially by direct perception. In *Samadhi* the same result is brought about in a controlled and scientific manner and the perception is therefore full and free from defects. The very nature of all spiritual facts of existence is such that they cannot be known by any other method. Those who seek for the ultimate secrets of the universe through telescopes and the ultimate secrets of human life through microscopes can, by the very nature of things, never succeed.

As intuition is the faculty of direct perception without the help of intermediate instruments, it is free from the inevitable distorting influence and error introduced by the vehicles of consciousness. All the imperfection which may be present in its exercise is due to the defective medium of the mind through which it is exercised and the knowledge is interpreted.

If this is pure and harmonized, its lack of development does not matter, except when the results of this perception have to be interpreted and formulated in terms of the intellect for communication to others. Many saints who were highly developed spiritually were illiterate. The lack of a trained intellect prevented them from interpreting and conveying satisfactorily the truths of the inner life to others, but it did not affect their perception of these truths.

The effectiveness of the intuitive faculty depends upon its penetrating power. The more penetrating its perception, called *Viveka-khyati* in the *Yoga-Sutras,* the deeper the realities which it can perceive and the more comprehensive its vision. The acme of its penetrating power is reached when it can penetrate through all the complexities and bewildering variety of manifested existence and *perceive* all things as derived from and existing in the One Reality. The unfoldment of intuition is thus not a question of putting together or building up something but that of sharpening the power of perception, so that it can cut through the jungle of illusions and obstructions which obscure our spiritual vision. That is why purification, renunciation, and harmonization play a more important part in treading the path of Holiness than does the acquisition of knowledge.

Since intuition plays such an important part in meditation it will be worthwhile dwelling for a while on the manner in which intuitive knowledge appears in consciousness in the early stages. Direct perception of the realities of spiritual life in the fullest sense takes place only in *Samadhi* but the aspirant need not wait for that advanced stage of yogic training for gaining some qualitative experience of intuitive knowledge. It is possible to have definite experiences of this kind of knowledge provided the conditions for the functioning of the intuitive faculty are present to some extent at least. In fact, it is not only possible but necessary to have this kind of experience because it shows us that the channel between our spiritual and intellectual natures has begun to open up and the real purpose of meditation is being fulfilled at least partially.

There is something extraordinarily heartening in having even occasional experiences of this nature because they assure us definitely that there is an inexhaustible source of spiritual knowledge within us and it is possible for us to draw upon that source by progressive attunement to it. We, of course, believe in all this as a theoretical possibility but it is quite a different thing to realize that our belief has a basis in fact and it is possible to put it to practical use. With this definite assurance we turn increasingly inward for everything we need for our spiritual progress and thus is laid the foundation of the true occult life—centered in our Divinity.

To understand how the intuitive faculty functions in the earlier stages of spiritual progress it is necessary to have some idea of the difference between spiritual knowledge as it exists on the planes of Spirit and as it appears on the planes of the lower mind. On the higher planes it is unencumbered by the lower mind and exists in its *Svarupa* or true form. On the lower planes it is clothed in the lower mind and can exist only in its *Rupa* or in the form of concepts and ideas. Therefore, when spiritual knowledge descends into the realm of the lower mind it must assume a concept or set of ideas as a body, just as the *Atma* or the Spirit must take up a body when it has to function on the physical plane. Under these conditions the true spiritual knowledge serves as a soul of the intellectual concept present in the lower mind. But there is a tremendous difference between such a concept ensouled and irradiated by spiritual knowledge and a concept formed by the mind as a result of mere intellectual study and devoid of any spiritual insight. The former is living, dynamic and of great significance to the aspirant. The latter is a mere collection of ideas, divorced from life and incapable of providing any inspiration or satisfaction to the individual.

The above considerations provide an explanation of the manner in which knowledge of a spiritual nature generally wells up from within as a result of the functioning of the intuitive faculty. It seems to come from nowhere, without any warning, and in its first impact on the mind appears to be a mere void, without form or substance. But very quickly it seems to crystallize into a pattern consisting of ideas which give it a mental form and serve to embody its significance.

In this manner of its expression in the lower mind one is reminded of a rocket in fireworks which shoots up into the sky as if from nowhere and then bursts into a shower of colored sparks shining beautifully against the dark background. At one moment it is a mere streak of light in the sky, heralding an exquisite display of light and color, and at another it has transformed itself into a display of scintillating stars in the sky, revealing the splendor which was hidden within its bosom.

It is characteristic of intuitive knowledge which appears in this manner that it should be caught in a mental receptacle immediately, the moment it makes its first impact on the mind. All that is necessary for this is to direct the mind to it with full attention. It then records and gives shape to itself naturally, rapidly and effortlessly. This effortless and lucid expression reveals its intuitive origin and is a part of its inherent nature. But the expression needs an alert and receptive mind which is ready and competent to give it a suitable shape and keep itself out of the picture for the time being. The poet must convert it immediately into a beautiful song, the musician into a symphony, the mathematician into a theorem, the philosopher into a concept, the artist into a concrete form. Any delay or lack of attention means almost certainly that the heavenly visitor will turn back and depart and perhaps make his visits less frequently.

The mode of influx hinted at above is only one of the ways in which intuitive knowledge may appear within the mind of the aspirant. The ways of the Spirit are mysterious and unpredictable and don't always conform to a set pattern, nor are all such communications associated with the same degree of intensity or enlightenment. But every time knowledge descends from those high realms the hallmark of the Spirit is there and the recipient can always recognize it. There can be no confusion or bewilderment when the Spirit communicates, but only enlightenment, though of different degrees depending upon the capacity of the receiver.

Knowledge which appears in this manner should not be confused with experiences of a psychic nature which take the form of visions and sounds of various kinds and have their origin in the psychic nature of man. Though generally spectacular, these lack the reliability and certainty associated with all manifestations of the Spirit. The fact that they frequently result in excitement and vainglorious ideas about one's spiritual progress is enough to show their lower origin. All expressions of the Spirit are associated with an indescribable imperturbability and impersonality and though there is an influx of peace and power there is no excitement of any kind.

4.

Christian Meditation and Contemplation

JOHN BRIAN PARRY

One of the major barriers in communication is the widely differing meanings placed upon words by different individuals. The word "meditation" is an example. In many systems meditation includes concentration, reflection, and contemplation. There are often intermediate states.

Christian Meditation

In general Christian usage, meditation means one of the lower reaches of prayer. The Oxford Dictionary of the Christian Church defines meditation as "mental prayer in its discursive form. It is the type of mental prayer appropriate to beginners and as such accounted its lowest stage." In these terms meditation is a quiet reflective pondering on a chosen theme. The aim is to stimulate the will and to condition the emotions. Probably the best known of all Christian spiritual methods, the "Spiritual Exercises" of St. Ignatius Loyola, is based on the use of mental prayer in its discursive or reflective form. The imagination is deliberately used to vividly create a picture of the subject of the meditation. The memory, reason, and will are then brought to bear in tune on the subject. During the first of the four weeks necessary to fully carry out the "Spiritual Exercises" the subjects for meditation are all concentrated on sin and the utter vileness of the person concerned. The meditation on hell at the end of the first week is particularly hair-raising. As an instrument for creating obedience to superiors and personal self-discipline, Loyola's "Exercises" have not been bettered by the most modern methods of brainwashing. It is an interesting fact that they seem to enjoy less popularity in the atmosphere which Pope John and Vatican II released.

Meditation as a discursive form of mental prayer does have considerable value which should not be obscured if it has been, on occasions, misused. It may be used with profit by beginners in meditation as an aid to concentration. An example might be better than a description.

Take the story of the woman who had haemorrhages for twelve years, who was healed by Jesus (Luke 8: 42-48). One thinks of the crowd, the noise and smells of the Palestine street, the Master almost suffocated, the woman who had been ill for so long and whose property had been used up by unsuccessful medical treatment, the final hope in her mind, the touch on his garment. Jesus was so sensitive to real need that he was able to distinguish between the jostling crowd and the touch of faith on his garment. One pictures the cure and the conversation, and then with the experience of the whole story recreated in imagination, concentrates on a particularly important point and applies it to one's own life, e.g. the sensitivity of Jesus or the faith of the woman. Concentrating on virtues in this way and resolving to build them into one's life is one of the major ends of meditation used in the traditional Christian method. Indeed, this is where meditation for the vast majority of Christians has started and finished. Moral perfection was commanded by Jesus and all types of Christians have sought it.

Prayer

Beyond meditation, as normally described in Christian manuals of spirituality, there are other, higher types of prayer. These will be considered below; but first a preliminary word about prayer in general.

When the word "prayer" is used, many think immediately of petition. This is by far the most widely known and misused form of prayer. "Please God, give me . . ." or "Please God, do this . . ." While petition has a real place, it should be placed in its proper and wider context.

The Greek theologian and "Doctor of the Church," St. John of Damascus (c.675-c.749) in *De Fide Orthodoxa,* gave a definition of prayer which has never been challenged. Prayer, he says, is "the lifting up of the mind to God." By mind, he means much more than intellect; also included are the emotions and the faculty of spiritual vision.

The following prayer by the late John Baillie, a Presbyterian minister of the Church of Scotland, gives some idea of the scope and possibility of prayer:

> O God, who art from eternity unto eternity, and art not at one time in one place because all times and places are in Thee, I would now seek to understand my destiny as a child of Thine. Here I stand, weak and mortal amid the immensities of nature. But blessed be Thou, O Lord God, that Thou hast made me in Thine own likeness and hast breathed into me the breath of Thine own life. Within this poor body Thou hast set a spirit that is akin to Thine own Spirit. Within this corruptible Thou hast planted incorruption and within this mortal immortality. So from this little room and this short hour I can lift up my mind beyond all time and space to Thee, the uncreated One, until the light of Thy countenance illumines all my life.

Although different authors give various classifications, and at the risk of oversimplification, the following generalized classification of the stages or types of prayer may be useful. Comment will be made only on those which relate directly to meditation and contemplation.

1. **Vocal Prayer**

   a. Adoration of the God revealed in Jesus Christ, in the Church and sacraments, in men and in nature.

   b. Thanksgiving is the natural response for the "givenness" of God to man.

   c. Penitence or a realization of the gap between the perfection of God and the imperfection of the individual.

   d. Intercession or petition ideally is the lifting up of the person or circumstance to realization of the divine purpose.

2. **Mental Prayer**

   a. *Meditation or intellectual pondering* as described above. In Ascetical Theology this is usually held to correspond to the Purgative Way, the first of the three degrees of the spiritual life. The chief purpose is the identification and elimination of bad habits. The imagination and intellect are the chief instruments used.

   b. *Affective Prayer.* This is the beginning of the next degree, the Illuminative Way. In this degree the person is cleansed from attachment to all created things and enlightened (illumined) in the things of the spirit. Affective prayer is the use of the affections and the will. Paradoxically, deepening detachment from things and persons increases the capacity for love. The expanding love of God results in an expanded ability to love one's fellows.

c. *The Jesus Prayer.* Some mention must be made of a form of prayer developed in and still widely used by the Eastern Orthodox Church and now receiving widespread attention in the Western Church. This prayer form is so ancient as to go back almost to Apostolic times. The actual words are simple: "Lord Jesus Christ, Son of God, have mercy on me, a sinner." But the spiritual exercises associated with it, called Hesychasm, are complex and intended to suit every need from that of the beginner to the highest spiritual attainment.

The prayer attempts to transform the individual who uses it. Its use should be approached with caution and moderation. Many writers warn that a spiritual director is essential if one is to use the prayer in a serious and sustained way, as it can cause profound psychological disturbance. The best protection in this as in most else will be simplicity of life and a high degree of self-awareness.

At first the prayer is repeated aloud a set number of times each day. This should be done alone and without being disturbed. During the repetition the attention should be held lightly on the words without any strained attempt to penetrate the meaning. One can sit upright in a comfortable position, stand, kneel, or lie prostrate, depending on one's temperament. The vocal use of the Jesus Prayer is regarded as building a desirable habit. The next step is to repeat the prayer silently an increased number of times during the day and night. Writing on the use of the Prayer, Bishop Ignatius Briarchanov says, "Experience will soon show that in using this method, especially at first, the words should be pronounced with extreme unhurriedness so that the mind may have time to enter the words as into forms." (Some writers suggest that the breath should be regulated so that one breathes in to the words "Lord Jesus Christ, Son of God" and out to the rest of the prayer. The regularity of breathing conjoined with the silent repetition of the prayer in the mind is a tried method of building concentration.)

The final stage is that the prayer is taken down into the heart. When this is achieved the relationship of individual and prayer is reversed. Instead of the individual's praying, the prayer now lives itself with every heart beat. Again to quote Briarchanov: "It is one thing to pray with attention with the participation of the heart; it is another thing to descend with the mind into the temple of the heart and from there offer mystical prayer filled with divine grace and power. The second is the result of the first. The attention of the mind during prayer draws the heart into sympathy. With the strengthening of the attention, sympathy of heart and mind is turned into union of heart and mind. Finally when attention makes the prayer its own, the mind descends into the heart for the most profound and sacred service of prayer."

The Jesus Prayer has been discussed at length because it is an example hallowed by long, almost, one could say, scientific usage of the deepening stages of prayer. Beginning with vocal, moving through meditation as sustained intellectual pondering, and coming to the use of the affections and the Illuminative Way. Finally, when the mind descends into the heart the way is open to Contemplation.

3. Contemplative Prayer

Christian theologians and mystics (the two are often closer than is commonly imagined) sometimes distinguish between two types of Contemplation. The first is the peak of Ascetical Theology and is often called "acquired contemplation." This is the highest to which an individual may attain by the full development of his natural powers. "Infused contemplation" is the second and is the subject of Mystical Theology. It is supposed to be the result of divine grace acting directly upon and within the human spirit. Both constitute the third degree of the spiritual life, the Unitive Way.

There are two levels of contemplative prayer which constitute "acquired contemplation." They are:

a. *The Prayer of Loving Regard.* This prayer or state is one of extreme interior simplicity. Intellectual striving and imaginative pictures have now been left behind. The mind possesses truth and contemplates it by a direct and simple act and enjoys it without effort. The key words are "contemplates without effort." Again, prayer at this level results in love. Sometimes this love, arising from the certainty of knowledge which contemplation gives, results in a colloquy which may or may not be spoken and which may even be written down. Thomas Merton, the Trappist monk, said: "When your tongue is silent, you can rest in the silence of the forest. When your imagination is silent, the forest speaks to you, tells you of its unreality and of the Reality of God. But when your mind is silent, then the forest becomes magnificently real and blazes transparently with the Reality of God: for now I know that the Creation which first seems to reveal Him, in concepts, then seems to hide Him, by the same concepts, finally is REVEALED IN HIM, in the Holy Spirit; and we who are in God find ourselves united, in Him, with all that springs from Him. This is prayer, and this is glory!"

In this lofty state of contemplation there is only one reality—that which is perceived. Because the perceiver does not attempt to clothe the perceived with descriptions or any concepts or classifications from his own limited self-experience, and allows it to be itself, naked and pure, so in our usual egocentric terms there is no perceiver—only the object of perception—the act of perception. As Merton says above, "This is prayer, and this is glory!"

But there are still more rarified levels to be attained.

b. *The Prayer of Faith,* often called the Prayer of Darkness. It is almost impossible to find expressions which convey accurately anything of the Prayer of Faith to those who are not versed in contemplation, and experienced contemplatives do not need descriptions. Any concept is likely to mislead. A good guide at this level in Christian literature is *The Cloud of Unknowing,* written in England by an anonymous author, probably in the 14th century. The cloud of unknowing is a cloud between a man and God. When asked the question, "How am I to think of God himself, and what is He?" the author simply replies, "I do not know." The reality of God, whatever it or he may be, must be utterly beyond any concept, theology, idea, or title which the mind or imagination can frame. In Chapter Seven the author describes how thoughts of God, or questions about redemption and creation, are to be treated as distractions holding a man back from reality. There is only one way which will finally break through and that is love without concept or desire. "Strike that thick cloud of unknowing with the sharp dart of longing love, and on no account whatever think of giving up."

As a contemplative penetrates ever deeper into the Darkness of Unknowing, he gradually comes to what another mystic, John Ruysbroeck, has beautifully described: "In this darkness there shines and is born an incomprehensible light, which is the Son of God, in Whom we behold eternal life. And in this Light one becomes seeing; . . . in the idle emptiness in which the spirit has lost itself through fruitive love, and where it receives without means the brightness of God, and is changed without interruption into that brightness it receives."

According to most descriptions we have now left Ascetical Theology and acquired contemplation far behind and are plumbing the obscure depths of Mystical Theology and infused contemplation. According to every major Christian contemplative—and they are the only Christian opinions worth having on this matter—there is a vast difference in nature between acquired and infused contemplation. The first is the work of man straining to the uttermost his natural capacities. The second, infused contemplation, is the action of God, working within a man.

For students of meditation and contemplation, this

distinction is of profound importance. It is perhaps the crossing-over point between Christian mysticism and that of Hinduism and Buddhism. It is
only at the apex of Christian experience that the
barrier between God and man is broken down. With
the exception of Eckhart, few Christians could af-
firm without some feeling of discomfort the ancient
Hindu statement, "Thou art That."

Christian thought has always been essentially dual-
istic even whilst the primacy and oneness of God
has been proclaimed. God and the universe stand
apart from each other. Although theologians have
never satisfactorily explained how the gulf between
God and his creation came into being, they are at
one in proclaiming that a bridge was made by God
in Jesus Christ. The actual reason why God did this
is still in dispute. The mystics seem to support this
when they speak of infused contemplation. This is
the work of God, pure and simple, operating directly on the humble and loving soul as a free and un-
earned gift. In a mysterious way God inhabits and
enlivens his image and likeness which is a man. In
Eckhart's famous words, "Here man has won again
what he eternally is and ever shall be. Here God is
received into the soul."

A Small Caution

Any serious practice of meditation enhances a
man's sensitivity to life. This can mean greater understanding, increased vitality, a more vivid appre-
hension of beauty. For some people, however, the
reaction is in terms of a lower form of psychism.
They levitate or see clairvoyant visions, hear celestial
music, or hold conversations with discarnate entities
either as mediums or, more often, through automatic
writing.

There is no need for alarm if these phenomena occur. The danger arises if one takes them seriously. Ascetical Theology deals extensively, and sometimes quaintly, with the various manifestations of this level of psychism. It also clearly points out the remedy in a characteristic manner. If prayer is the lifting up of the mind to God, then a true contemplative will not, indeed cannot, be satisfied with anything less than God. All discoveries on the path to God are to be put aside along with concepts and ideologies if the goal is to be reached. Unfortunately, some manuals on meditation now available fail to sound this caution. A few even seem to regard psychism as the goal. Truly, they give a stone in place of bread.

A Rich Heritage

The current revival of popular interest in meditation and contemplation is a very healthy sign. It is, especially in cultures which have been heavily industrialized and affluence-oriented, probably an inevitable reaction to a century where man's main focus of attention has been on objects and their use for personal or national advantage. Although there are some notable exceptions, most of these cultures have been nominally Christian. There has thus been a tendency to ignore some of the rich heritage which Christian contemplatives have left and are still creating. This reaction is natural but unfortunate. Men such as John, Paul, Dionysius the Areopagite, Cassiar, Clement of Alexandria, Origen, John of the Ladder, Augustine, Bernard, Eckhart, Catherine of Siena, Catherine of Genoa, Boehme, Tauler, John Ruysbroeck, Walter Hilton, Teresa of Avila, John of the Cross, William Law, all were mystics of the first order. And these are only a few names on a very long list. Translations of some of their writings are readily available in most major languages. In English, extracts from their major works are included in inexpensive anthologies. Every person interested in meditation and contemplation will welcome the increasing cross-fertilization of insights and methods between the great religions of the world. However, it would be a pity if the substantial contribution from Christian sources were not used or appreciated.

Although much Christian attention on meditation and contemplation has, over the long centuries, been directed mainly to monks and nuns living under some form of enclosure, there has always been an awareness that essentially they are for everyman. Contemplation is not a luxury confined to the solitary few. It is equally for the involved many.

Contemplation demands solitude and silence, but this does not necessarily mean an absence of other people. Solitude and silence are conditions within one. They are found whenever one turns his attention away from things, including his own prejudices and opinions, and begins to withdraw into the silent temple which is in each human heart.

Thomas Merton describes the process of interior silence as ". . . shutting up and emptying my mind and leaving the inner door open for the Holy Spirit to enter from the inside, all the doors being barred and all my blinds down."

5.

The Art of Meditation

FELIX LAYTON

Meditation is an art.

He who truly meditates is an artist.

His meditation is a thing of beauty and a source of strength and understanding.

Yet the quality and style of meditation is unique to each artist. This is so because in his highest nature the artist in meditation sees the one, all-embracing wisdom, light and love, which is always the same. But he brings the vision and knowledge of it through his brain and personality which is unique to him. This stamps the meditation with all that is uniquely beautiful in his personality.

This personality is capable of expressing beauty or ugliness, understanding or prejudice, love or hate. When the one manifests through him in meditation it touches and strengthens all the finest qualities and weakens their opposites. One might say that in meditation the one breath sweeps through the musical instrument of the personality. As it does so it sounds the notes of that unique personality, strengthening the beauties and harmonies and tuning out the discords.

Each artist has his own style which a connoisseur will recognize in a picture whether it be a landscape, a portrait or an abstract. A great musician's unique style will show through whether the composition be a march, a nocturne or a symphony. It will be recognized by one who knows the art of music.

In his early development an artist usually studies in an art school or under a teacher from whom he learns techniques—the "science of his art." As he studies, a teacher may point out that the student could better get the effect he is striving for if he did certain things. Perhaps the teacher advises him to make a certain line stronger or eliminate a figure here or change a color there. These ideas are helpful at first while the student is mastering the techniques of his art. He may profit greatly by copying the works of the masters of his art. But later, as the student's capacity and uniqueness develop, he will say to advisors "No. That line is how I want it." "I need that figure" or "A change in color would not harmonize with my idea." Eventually, although he admires and loves his teachers for the help they have given and the techniques he has learned from them, he reaches a stage where he must go alone and express his unique art. So it is with meditation.

Styles of art change. Art schools of Europe, India, China, and Egypt have put their stamp on all the works of a certain period or location. So in the art of meditation, styles often connected with religions such as Christianity (exalted prayer), Buddhism, Islam, or with nations such as Japan, India, or Tibet, may dominate a large group or school. But within that school each eventually develops his own unique style.

We see a world in transition today. We see a mixing of races, cultures, religions, social patterns, and all aspects of man's life. These forces are producing entirely new patterns everywhere. The same is true in the field of meditation, for we see all over the country students of Zen, Buddhist, Vedanta, Sufi, and Christian schools of meditation. And we see students studying in one school, then moving to another as they feel the need for different techniques. And just as the cultural blending is not producing a conglomorate, but an entirely new culture, so this blending of techniques of meditation is producing an entirely new school of meditation. This new school, when developed, will stamp its fundamental style on all the uniquely beautiful creations of its new artists of meditation.

Perhaps one characteristic of the new school will be the approach to the One through the beauties of nature. Awareness of the wonder which is a tree or a sunset, comes through an awareness of the glory and beauty of the life behind the form and through the awakening within man's consciousness of an inner sensitivity and awareness without which the outer beauty cannot be perceived.

Another characteristic which is developing among the wise young radicals in the field of meditation is a stressing that meditation must result in action. It has always been recognized that effective meditation must result in action. To be aware of great realities in meditation is to produce in the daily life an urge to act, to bring those realities into manifestation. In older schools there has often been a tendency to minimize the physical activity by living in retirement in a monastery or hermitage, but the follower of the emerging school of meditation has strong contacts with the world's activities, and his meditations with nature, for instance, will result in active work to prevent pollution and to conserve nature's beauties. Contact in meditation with an inner harmony where separation, conflict and hate are unknown, produces action to bring social justice and peace to the world. At first this may result in "militant pacifist" actions but as more and more contact the realities of inner peace, and cease to think in terms of conflict, these young people, whose thoughts will not countenance oppression and war, will be powerful instruments in bringing justice and peace to the world.

The creative arts involve contacting a source of inspiration which transcends the mind, and bringing it to expression in the material world in terms of line, color, movement, sound or whatever medium is chosen. To many this is exactly what happens through meditation. To them meditation is the art of stilling the mind and the whole personality so that the individual, in full waking consciousness, is aware of the center of stillness and power which is the heart of his being. He then allows this to express itself in beautiful actions in the world around him. To such the approach to meditation as an art is more natural and productive of results than the approach to it as a science. To them the techniques of meditation learned from a school or teacher are the scientific tools of meditation. But the unconscious use of these skills in a beautiful act is the art and crowning glory of meditation.

6.

Spiritual Experience--
Illusion or Reality?

V. WALLACE SLATER

Communication with Higher Powers

Throughout the ages there have been men and women who have claimed to be able to contact unseen beings, spirits, or supernatural powers, for answers to problems which could not be resolved by normal reasoning. The idea of an oracle, as a place, person, or object, dates from remote antiquity. The ancient Greeks consulted their deities for advice or prophecy through a person specially prepared by ritual bathing, anointing, and self-discipline, in a special place—often a cave—called the oracle, where the advice was received in the form of a spoken word or as an inner conviction. The Hebrew spiritual communications were by "word of mouth" as when God spoke to Moses.

Mohammed, worried about the poor condition of Arabs, their ignorance and superstition, spent several years in meditation on the problem and received a "call" to be a prophet and teacher for his race. How he received that call we do not know, but his followers have always claimed that he was "inspired of God."

Throughout the history of the Christian church devoted men and women have claimed to have seen and heard intermediaries between God and man: the Virgin Mary and the Saints. Outstanding examples were the voices of Joan of Arc, the appearance of the Virgin Mary to Bernadette at Lourdes and of the infant Jesus to St. Therese of Lisieux.

Whatever the age or the religion the approach has usually included some form of preparation for control of mind and body: bathing, fasting, long hours at prayer, asceticism and such like.

More recently spirit guides have been consulted, the spirits of people who have recently died, or of persons long dead but of glamorous origin such as Red Indians, Chinese, Tibetan lamas, African witch doctors, Indian yogis. The assumption is that when a person dies, his spirit is suddenly possessed of divine wisdom, including a knowledge of future events.

It is natural to ask how genuine any of the claims have been. Were the prophets and seers self-deluded or just charlatans, or did they feel inspired and invent the "talking with God" idea from genuinely good motives to encourage obedience to moral law by their followers?

The word Theosophy has been defined as Divine Wisdom, implying that at some stage in human evolution man has been able to commune with God. Mme. H. P. Blavatsky, however, pointed out that, when she used the term, she did not mean wisdom of God, but wisdom of the gods, that is the wisdom possessed by the hierarchy of superhuman beings, including men made perfect in a former world period, Dhyan Chohans, and the creators of the phenomenal universe, Dhyani Buddhas.

She amplified this by adding that such wisdom could be attained by metaphysical processes. Since the infinite cannot be known by the finite self, she affirmed that divine wisdom can be communicated only to the higher spiritual Self in a state of ecstasy. Real ecstasy was defined by Plotinus as "the liberation of the mind from the finite consciousness, becoming one and identified with the infinite." It is that state known in India as *samadhi,* the climax of meditation in raja yoga.

Since H. P. B. made claims to metaphysical knowledge, and expressed the wish to help others to that knowledge, it was natural that the practice of meditation should have played an important part in the daily life of members of The Theosophical Society.

No Short Cuts

All teachers of yoga and meditation have emphasized that there are no short cuts. Yoga is not a short, quick, easy route to success or to a phenomenal memory, or to divine knowledge. No one can get something for nothing. The first requirement for any form of spiritual development is to initiate controlled changes in consciousness and character by moral and ethical training, by the mastery of sensuous desires—not their suppression, but their control —so that one is not misled by the impressions of the senses. All this is then followed by control of the mind itself, elimination of prejudices and avoidance of hasty unbalanced judgments. Then one can hope to transcend the mind to that suprarational state referred to by H. P. B. as "metaphysical knowledge."

Such careful preparation is irksome in an age of short cuts. People want to be able to learn without effort—a tape-recorder playing to the ears during sleep and such like. Students will pay large sums for an amulet which will assure them success in an examination. Drugs are taken to produce a superconscious state which, it is hoped, will lead to contact with higher powers, to illumination, a short cut to wisdom.

There are many cults of meditational practices ranging from extreme asceticism and discipline to no discipline at all. One school gives each member a mantra specially designed for his own use to suit his temperament and personality. By repeating or chanting the mantra, the phrase of words, either in English or in an ancient language, it is claimed that one can transcend the mind. It cannot be denied that some such chanting, when performed with right intent, can produce a wonderful effect. It may relax the mind and produce a sense of peace and good will. Can it give illumination, divine wisdom, or is the mind repressed by autohypnotism? A mind repressed or transcended? Illusion or reality, hallucination or Self-realization? No one can answer the question for another.

The Real from the Unreal

Whatever the method used for the training and practice of meditation, we have to recognize the possibility of mental delusion, which can arise in many ways, such as:

1. The unconscious prejudices arising from early training, or racial and national history, as when a mystic receives an inspired message in accord with the tenets of his particular religious sect.

2. A desire to believe something, for example that a beloved friend, on the other side of death, is communicating with one.

3. The blind acceptance of a revered leader's statements, that appear to be confirmed by the devotee's own inspiration during meditation.

The confirmation or the illumination may appear as an inner voice, which is so real as to appear objective, or as a vision, even during waking consciousness, or as a dream following a session of deep meditation.

In the first place let us face the fact that we may not be able to know the difference between illusion and reality, and so the first rule for their differentiation should be not to be too gullible. If the inspiration appears to be helpful then let us not tell others that we have had a spiritual experience, using that as authority to get them to believe and follow us. Let the experience be held lightly without self-elevation or spiritual pride.

There are some safeguards that can be applied to avoid an illusory inspirational experience. The first and most important one is to eliminate self, the lower self. The first step in meditation is concentration, fixing the mind one-pointedly on a subject so that the subject merges into one's inner consciousness to give a clarity of understanding that a wandering mind cannot reach. But we have then to ask ourselves, what is the motive? Is it truly impersonal or is it that we want to inflate our ego, to be more efficient as a personal adornment?

One of the preliminary requirements for raja yoga is the obligation to self-study. This means thinking about oneself in the sense of getting to know one's own character, one's strengths and one's weaknesses; learning to know one's failings; learning to distinguish the self associated with selfishness from the real inner Self which is selfless.

With such preparation one should be able to distinguish an inspiration or an intuition that is untinged by self and which is therefore probably REAL from ideas triggered off by thoughts of self, whether consciously or unconsciously, such ideas having greater possibility of being illusory.

A second safeguard against illusion is to transcend the mind, a most difficult task. In the broad exercise of meditation, concentration fixes the mind on the subject, meditation leads the mind around the subject to understand it, contemplation (*samadhi* or ecstasy) takes consciousness beyond the mind. In theosophical terms this means *buddhi*, but in the language of yoga philosophy it is *atma*, the level of man's highest principle, the will.

It is the elevation of consciousness beyond the mind to which H. P. Blavatsky refers in her *Glossary*, where she speaks of meditation as a means of attaining spiritual liberation. Her definition continues that psycho-spiritual powers are thereby obtained, inducing a state of ecstasy leading to a clear and correct perception of the eternal truths, in both the visible and the invisible universe.

In very broad terms these truths include the idea of "an omnipresent, eternal, boundless and immutable Principle, on which all speculation is impossible" and the idea of "the fundamental identity of all Souls with the Universal Over-Soul." Such an oversoul is at the level of *atma* as mentioned above. These truths may be just intellectual philosophical ideas. The practice of meditation can make of them living realities.

Let us therefore examine this goal of all meditational practices, a goal which can take us beyond illusion to reality.

Samadhi

Put very briefly the philosophy on which *samadhi* (contemplation) is based is the *buddhi-manas* (intuition-higher mind, or the illumined mind), is the Higher Self, the spirit of man which continues to exist after the death of his lower vehicles.

Atma is both universal and individual. Thus man, through his highest principle, *atma,* is rooted in the Universal Self, or Spirit of the Universe, and yet he also has an individual existence in his own Higher Self, *buddhi-manas.* It is the principle of *atma* which gives *buddhi-manas* an identity as a spiritual consciousness, in which *atma,* will, manifests as judgment, discrimination.

If we could transcend the limitations of the individual self at this highest level of individual consciousness we should indeed be beyond illusion. We should be *Mahatmas,* beyond *atma*; the individual consciousness would have merged into the Universal Self.

Let us now look at this mystical experience and ask ourselves how far can we go in thinking that we can thus contact reality, and to what extent can we rely upon any inspiration or intuition that we may experience?

Looking at it from the materialistic or physical body point of view, there is no doubt that an exercise in yoga meditation, based on personal effort and sincerity, and which proceeds along the lines laid down by tradition, can lead to an unbiased illumination. The traditional method is an all-round process from the preparatory stage of moral discipline to final contemplation as set out in the eight steps of raja yoga: twofold moral and ethical requirements (self-restraint and self-discipline); control of the physical body; control of breathing, not forced, but steady, full and relaxed; control of the senses with ability to withdraw consciousness from their domination; and the threefold control of the mind by concentration, meditation and contemplation.

Still taking a materialistic viewpoint, such an ordered approach to a state of complete relaxation at all levels of consciousness, physical, emotional, and

mental, must result in the ability to find answers
to problems, to make judgments and to arrive at
decisions that will be impersonal, lucid, and logical.
They will certainly be nearer to reality than hasty
conclusions arrived at while distracted by bodily irritations, emotional disturbances, or excitement and
mental prejudices and preconceptions.

However, theosophical philosophy is not based on
purely materialistic ideas of man and the universe.
It holds that man is a spirit and if we can lift our
consciousness to that spiritual level, then, even if we
do not reach absolute reality, we certainly approach
nearer to it. This thought and hope leads to a need
to know something of that final stage of meditation
called *samadhi*.

The word *samadhi* means literally "directing together," that is, uniting in a positive, directed manner. Thus the lower and higher selves are united
into a "wholeness," a unity of spirit at all levels of
consciousness. All one's faculties are collected into
union with the very essence of being, sometimes
called be-ness, which is even above man's highest
principle, *atma*. This means losing the consciousness of the individual, our own individuality, and
becoming One with all other selves, through the
Universal Over-Self. One is then impersonally aware
of that eternal, boundless, and immutable principle.

Having reached this state one ceases to think, one
becomes. This is not easy. We may just enter that
state by a point of our consciousness for a fraction
of time. If we *think* we are in a state of *samadhi*,
then, by that very thinking we cease to be there—
our consciousness has dropped back into the thinking
level.

That state of *samadhi* is better described as supra-
consciousness rather than superconsciousness. "Su-
per" implies above; "supra" implies all-embracing,

above and below, within and without. In that state one becomes omnipresent, omniscient, and omnipotent at a subtle level of consciousness, but one is self-less, having become "All-Self" as one with the Self of the Universe.

The following quotation from Mr. N. Sri Ram (*The Theosophist,* February 1968) expresses in concise form all that this article has attempted to convey.

> Theosophy is a Wisdom which goes beyond the mind. Such Wisdom is possible to man, because in his inner nature, in the basic consciousness which is moulded into a particular mind, there is a power to change himself, to free his mind from its conditioning, even from the very possibility of being conditioned, by the factors which operate upon it.
>
> The mind becomes a pure mind. It is Intelligence itself, not limited by ideas from its past. Such an intelligence can know the inward truth underlying the exterior forms and experience of the forms.

7.

The Placid Lake of the Mind

HELEN V. ZAHARA

According to ancient tradition, the personality in which each one of us lives is only a small part of our true nature; beneath the facade which we display there are depths of being in which are locked the untapped potential of the spiritual Self, the immortal, enduring part of ourselves. Unfortunately, we are caught up so much of the time with the pressures, demands, attractions, sorrows, pains, and excitements of daily life that most of us have little time to think about the unseen part of ourselves or even perhaps to be aware of the existence of any consciousness beyond our sensations, feelings, and thoughts. Yet, if the ancient tradition be true, we are only really partly living if we do not open the inner portal that reveals the Self within, not only to discover its reality, but also to permit it to have expression in our lives. Furthermore, the Self, according to the same tradition, is not an isolated entity, but is rooted in the one Divine Consciousness which pervades and sustains the universe and all its creatures. What a tremendous concept! What infinite power and beauty may be discovered and brought into action, if we but begin the inner search and penetrate beyond the outer personality to the depths within.

To begin this process is one of the functions of meditation. It is a technique of self-exploration leading to the experience of heightened and expanded awareness, which is beyond the area of psychism or drug-induced changes of consciousness. It involves the opening of one's heart and the turning of one's mind in new directions, giving time to commune with oneself, with nature, and with life around. This may require the breaking down of old patterns of thinking and feeling and therefore it is not a simple undertaking.

Meditation has other functions also, including the directing of thought to help others, and for healing. In addition, it has value in the development of a new sense of serenity and inward peace, a feeling of greater strength to meet the problems and stresses of each day, seeing things from a broader perspective, finding new values and meanings.

Whether meditation is undertaken for self-exploration or for other purposes such as have been mentioned, it involves bringing the mind first into a state of freedom, from which can proceed either creative and abstract thought, or a state of stillness in which the thinking process ceases, allowing intuition and new insights to arise from the deeper part of the Self. For many people it is not an easy practice. It depends on the individual's temperament, his one-pointedness, his interest, his circumstances, and his earnestness.

Some people think that meditation should be free and unstructured. Inward experience can arise spontaneously in a mind that is silent and alert, that does not exclude anything, but merges, as it were, with the life around. There can be exaltation also in awareness of nature and its beauties or in the in-

spiration of great music and art. It can happen at
various brief moments in the day without any set
discipline.

On the other hand, as a regular daily practice, meditation has great value if a few minutes can be set
aside for this purpose, perhaps in the morning before
the rush and activity of the day begin. One needs
to have a quiet place, free from disturbance, and
begin to bring the mind to a state of rest. Unfortunately, this is where the troubles of many people,
who undertake this practice, commence. As soon as
they sit down to meditate they find that the mind
will not be still, it is caught up in turmoil, in in-
consequential, superficial daydreams; it is filled with
fears, worries, memories, and anticipations; it is like
a butterfly, flitting from one point to another; it is
clouded by biases, prejudices, and doubts. So there
come frustration, disappointment and discourage-
ment and, despite all the beautiful statements that
are said about meditation, nothing happens.

That this is an age-old problem is clear from some
of the yoga writings. In *The Bhagavad Gita* Arjuna
cries out to his Guru: "Manas (the mind) is very
restless, it is impetuous, strong and difficult to bend;
I deem it as hard to curb as the wind." Then the
answer comes from the teacher Krishna: "Without
doubt, Manas is hard to curb and restless; but it
may be curbed by constant practice and dispassion."

About three centuries B.C. the great Indian sage
Patanjali described the turbulence of the mind as
"the modifications of the mind." He gave his famous teaching, which is as applicable today as it was
so many centuries ago. What must be achieved, he
taught, is the "inhibition of the modifications of the
mind." If that is reached, "then the Seer is established in his own essential and fundamental Nature."
But how to do this? There are many helpful meth-

ods, but Patanjali's classic system of Raja Yoga, as set out in his Yoga Sutras, still stands as one of the most valuable. In a simplified form it can be a very useful guide for the Western mind, especially for the beginner. Perhaps this is because the various steps prescribed are so logical.

Patanjali prescribed eight *angas* or aids. The first of these is concerned with a clean moral life, for obviously one's aims must be based on right ethics if one is to undertake a spiritual discipline, which is what meditation really is. It cannot be achieved for selfish reasons. So we find prescribed five self-restraints: one must abstain from injury to others through thought, word, or deed; from falsehood, from stealing, from passions and lust, and from avarice.

The second *anga* has been described as self-culture; there are five observances: external and internal purification, contentment, austerity, study, and devotion to God. This means that the individual undertaking this practice is turning his thoughts in the direction of the goal of yoga, which is union, in consciousness, with the Supreme.

The third *anga* is given as right posture. While those who are practiced in the East would use the lotus posture, the main need is to be seated in an upright position with head, neck, and back in a straight line. Then comes the fourth *anga* which is breath control. Again, if one is going deeply into yoga there are special exercises, but one can proceed with even breathing which will slow down naturally to the rate which occurs during sleep. Next there is what is called "sense withdrawal," which can perhaps be interpreted to mean the withdrawal of one's attention from objects and ideas which impinge upon the mind through the senses. If one's eyes are open one can be distracted by various things around. If one is disturbed by extraneous noise, it is difficult to concentrate. As suggested already, therefore, the aspirant should find a quiet place, free from disturbance, and then, seated in a comfortable posture, withdraw his awareness from the world without, turning his attention completely and utterly to the practice of introspection, directing his consciousness to the world within.

The first five *angas* are known as the external aids to yoga, and constitute preparation for the internal steps which now follow. In Patanjali's system we find three more *angas* given, and these really constitute the heart of the yoga practice. Although separately stated for the purpose of study they actually merge one into the other, and are not distinct and separate. These *angas* are stated as concentration (*dharana*), meditation (*dhyana*) and contemplation (*samadhi*).

When one tries to meditate one can understand why Patanjali began his system with concentration. I have already mentioned the turbulence of the mind, which is so difficult to curb. One way in which to bring it to a point where there is some control is to concentrate on something, thus confining the mind within a chosen area. One can concentrate on an inanimate or animate object; it can be a concept or aphorism; it can be a mantram which is repeated. Again it depends on one's temperament, but as far as my own limited experience goes, I find it helpful to choose something which has its own element of beauty. It can be a delicate flower, for instance, or a sparkling crystal—something which draws an aesthetic response. Of course it can also be something quite prosaic such as a matchbox or a stone. Each one can experiment for himself and find out whether there is some particular object which helps in the concentration process. Having decided on the object of concentration, place it before the mind's eye. If it is a physical object, observe it very carefully and in detail before closing the eyes, and then hold it in the mind. If it is something intangible, such as an aphorism or a concept, it can be read or repeated and then taken into one's mind. To concentrate on something in this way means focusing one's full attention upon it. From the state of concentration one moves gradually into the deepening process of meditation and contemplation.

To understand the movement of consciousness which can occur let us follow in imagination what may happen to a person who begins this practice. As an example let us say that an aspirant has decided to concentrate on an amethyst stone, which he may happen to have. When he starts thinking about it, he does not bring his mind to a halt, but he is directing it along a deliberately chosen channel. He thinks of the amethyst in all its aspects—its hardness, its weight, its facets, its deep rich purple color which sparkles in the light. He may imagine it lying in the earth, perhaps for millenia. He becomes absorbed in the jewel and all its aspects to such an extent that he shuts out all the other thoughts which are clamoring for attention, the irrelevancies, the day-dreams, the worries, the distractions which normally impinge upon his thinking. He is thus taking the first step in becoming master of his mind. Up to this point, he is analyzing, he is aware of facts regarding the jewel, and his mind is simply working at the analytical, concrete level, which in theosophical terminology is called lower mind, or lower *manas*.

Gradually, if he is successful in the process, he begins to change the level of his thinking, taking it up into more abstract realms (higher mind or *manas*). He becomes aware of the beauty of the amethyst, he may begin to think about its qualities and characteristics; a sense of wonder begins to arise as he considers the many processes which have gone into its making, realizing its relationship with the earth and other elements, thinking of its archetype of perfection which perhaps exists in the Universal Mind. Now there develops a steady flow of creative thought with regard to the stone, which invests it with new meaning. Somehow the individual begins to know the amethyst in a new way, to feel its life, so that he merges his own consciousness with it, and it is no longer just an object outside of himself. Without pausing he may move into a state of meditation, by which the knower and the known become one, separateness disappears, and there is a new sense of unity, an expansion of consciousness. There is a breaking down of the usual barriers of time and space, and in that moment of absorption there may come a stillness of the mind, which is not negative or passive, but is dynamic and alert. This is the state of contemplation. Now, it is suggested, the image of the stone should be dropped altogether from the mind, while the mind remains in that still, absorbed, poised state of consciousness. The mind is now emptied of images and forms, and in that moment it is free and open to receive intimations from the inner world of the Self, to experience intuition, *buddhi*. To use a well known analogy, the mind is as a clear placid lake, able to reflect the divine consciousness from within. As the Taoist phrase goes: "Bide in silence, and the radiance of the spirit shall come in and make its home."

In that state of contemplation, which is a state of consciousness beyond form, the individual can have spiritual insight which, however brief, can transform his understanding, can expand his awareness, lifting him out of his usually limited field into a new vision and a realization of the deeper reality which exists within. It may not happen for a long time.

It requires constant practice, but if only the preliminary stages are reached, these can be helpful in the direction and control of the mind. Furthermore, the process is a never-ending one, and one should realize that there are various levels of *samadhi*. The experience mentioned in the example given above is but the beginning.

As already suggested, there are various valuable ways for beginning meditation. If one decides to concentrate on a flower, for instance, one can try to enter into its life and to know it from the inside, to feel its life, to become, as it were, the flower. One can sit under a tree and merge consciousness with that growing thing, as it stretches its limbs up toward the sun. Ernest Wood, in his book *Concentration*, suggests even entering into the consciousness of a cat: ". . . experience its sensitiveness, its beauty, its being in poise and motion." In yogic literature we find references to concentration on such things as the tip of the nose, the point midway between the eyebrows, the lotus in the heart, the image of the deity, and the breath coming in and going out. There are also different *mantras* to be chanted while concentrating on the Divine Being.

In some Buddhist schools we find among the classical objects of meditation such things as: earth (in the form of a heap of sand), water (a bowl full), air (in the sensation at the surface of the skin), fire (the flame of a candle), a small round disc (blue, yellow, red, or white), light (entering through a small hole in a dark room), space (the open, heavenly vault). In Tibetan yoga there are the symbolic designs known as *yantras* and *mandalas*. It is a vast subject, involving much study and practice.

Having developed the art of meditation with objective things, then the more abstract themes—aphorisms and concepts and virtues, which are also recommended—will be less difficult to tackle. In this approach there is an entering into the meaning, penetrating behind the words and ideas to the reality beyond. Another important practice is to begin to probe into one's own being, asking the question "Who am I?" and seeking to realize the spiritual Self, rooted in the universal life, until one can make the affirmation of one's unity with One Divine Consciousness: "I am That, That am I." In each case, after the flow of steady thought on the subject of meditation has been achieved, there can come that point which transcends thought, when consciousness moves into a formless state where the experience cannot be fully described in words.

Meditation is, of course, of value only if it brings a change of heart, if it develops new meanings, and helps one to act more from the center of oneself in daily life. It can bring new poise and inner peace, and therefore is of as much value to the man in the street as it is to the yogi who retires from worldly life to the ascetic life of the forest or cave.

Whenever, through meditation and with right aspiration, the mind of the seeker is brought to a placid state, like a clear and calm mountain pool, unruffled by the winds of anger or desire, or other disturbing elements, the mind will then be able to reflect in its depths the light of the spiritual Sun, and the aspirant will grow in spiritual insight and understanding.

8.

What Is Meditation?

SIMONS ROOF

The World of Meditation

Meditation has become a household word. It often spills out these days, especially among its newest discoverers, in a jumble along with such terms as guru, samadhi, Zen, mind expansion, psychedelic experience, and transcendental consciousness.

But what is meditation?

Does it help one, as its advocates claim, to gain greater self-control and to release new capacities and qualities of being? Does it enable one to become a "new person"—wiser, more loving, more concerned about and more responsible toward others? Can its "peak-experiences," in current terminology, lead one to the discovery of basic values and "self-actualization"?

The classical and contemporary literature on meditation, in both West and East, is vast to the point of being overwhelming. Meditation is usually described as a discipline, a method, a process—a way of using mind and heart. But it is generally taught within the larger framework of a psychology, a philosophy, or a religion.

Much of the ancient teaching, usually religious or philosophical, has fallen into general disuse while some of it seems to retain its original vitality. Many old schools of meditation have been periodically re-organized and revitalized, and from time to time strong new schools have emerged. Much of the traditional teaching, edited and modified for better or worse, has reappeared in new language, sometimes enticing with promises of far-out psychic powers and other superhuman endowments.

But much which is new, exciting, and significant in the world of meditation is in progress.

A group of eminent phychiatrists, for example, is devising and testing meditative techniques for use in psychotherapy. A group of psychologists, psychiatrists, sociologists, and clergymen has been experimenting with the use of certain hallucinogenic drugs in producing value-changing peak-experiences or mystic-type states of consciousness. Others have attempted to reinterpret, restate, or re-create some of the traditional techniques and meditation forms in the light of findings in such disciplines as physiology, psychology, psychiatry, sociology, theology, and philosophy. Some of the better known groups which offer meditation instruction, both within and outside of organized religion, report innovative and apparently promising new methods both in the teaching of meditation and in its practice.

"The best definition of meditation," it is commonly said, "is the act of meditation itself."

This is so, meditators say, because meditation yields a subjective experiential knowledge. This knowledge involves psychological processes, within the totality of one's being, which may occur at many levels of consciousness, often simultaneously, and in intricate relationships. Consider what may be involved, for instance, in the intellectual or intuitive grasp of a new dimension of love while at the same time experiencing the fact of loving and of being loved. Our language is not yet large enough, medita-

tors remind us, to indicate precisely many of our
subtler states of being and types and stages of consciousness.

But a working definition, while ultimately inade-
quate, is both useful and necessary. The following
definition of meditation attempts to take into account the fundamentals of both classical and contemporary concepts, hypotheses, and practices:

Meditation is the disciplined exercise of awareness, utilizing such processes as recollecting, imagin-
ing, and logically and creatively thinking, or intui-
tively perceiving, which leads to comprehension of a
subject within an inclusive conceptual framework.
It may be practiced at progressive levels of knowledge,
energy, and consciousness. It may have such immediate goals as the search for interior growth, freedom,
and creativity, personality development and integration, self-knowledge, more inclusive love, wisdom,
and will, or simply greater joy, peace, or compassion.

Such a final goal of meditation may make it sound
like a formula for the production of saints. The
evidence from the saints themselves, of course, indicates this may be so. But meditation has been equally
vital in the development of leaders in a major cross-
section of human activities, ranging through the arts
and sciences to business and government. Our concern here is with the common human potential—any
man at his best, and humanity at its best.

How worthwhile is meditation in terms of its immediate goals, of goals which seem reasonably achiev-
able, for many people, this side of samadhi or divine
union?

A Map of Meditation

The practice of meditation dates back . . . how
many thousands of years? Perhaps to some forgotten
ancestor of ours who first learned to prolong his at-

tention, calmly and creatively, on the awesome mystery of his own nature or the identity of Man, or on the terrifyingly vast question of What lies behind everything in existence.

Meditation was an established practice, we know, in the Vedic days of India. It was developed to a high point in China by the age of Lao-Tzu. It was known to the priests of Egypt. It existed in Greece before it was practiced by such philosophers as Socrates and Plato. It was familiar to the early teachers of Judaism. It was practiced by the founders and the founding fathers of the chief religions and their ablest followers.

History abounds with testimony to the paramount place of meditation.

"The uncontrolled mind does not guess that the spiritual self is present: how can it meditate?" the Bhagavad-Gita asks. "Without meditation, where is peace? Without peace, where is happiness?" "Right meditation" is one of the requirements of Buddha's Noble Eightfold Path. "Meditation is the clarifier of a beclouded mind," according to Tibetan teachings. "By attaining the height of meditation," Lao-Tzu declares, "we gain fullness of rest. Returning to the Source means rest . . . and the return according to destiny means the eternal; knowing the eternal means enlightenment." "This kind of knowledge," Plato says, "is a thing that comes in a moment like a light kindled from a leaping spark which, once it has reached the soul, finds its own fuel." "Meditation is the key to worship," the Sufi Dhu-al Nun explains, "that which unlocks the door and gives entrance into the presence of God."

"St. Paul reminds us that we, being planted in the likeness of God, may attain to a higher and truer vision," Meister Eckhart states. "For this St. Dionysius says we require three things. The first is possession of one's mind. The second is a mind that is free. The third is a mind that can see. How can we acquire this meditative mind? By a habit of mental concentration." St. Teresa's emphasis on the necessity of meditation typifies the testimony of many saints: "If you had asked me about meditation, I could have instructed you and advised anyone to practice it even though they do not possess the virtues, for this is the first step to obtaining them all; it is vital for all Christians to begin this practice."

A map of the world of meditation can be drawn most quickly, perhaps, by reference to the psychology of meditation. Against this, specific schools and types of meditation—and the use of specific meditation forms—may be more easily understood.

Five great steps lead to the subjective experiential knowledge of "ultimate wholeness." These five levels of consciousness are usually, but not always, consecutively achieved.

> *Concentration* is the use of the conscious mind, with the will holding awareness steadily to a subject.

> *Reflection* is the use of the conscious mind with some use of the subconscious—some facility to dig material out of the "buried life" underlying normal everyday consciousness.

> *Intuition* is the use of the conscious mind with some use of both the subconscious and the superconscious (the "heavenly stuff" of the superconscious works on the "earthly stuff" of the conscious and subconscious, to produce results which, while sometimes not immediately provable, seem eminently practicable and reasonable).

> *Contemplation* is the use of the conscious mind with some use of the superconscious (also

called the level of intuition, love and wisdom, the soul of Atman, the level of the transcendental).

Illumination is the perfected or nearly perfected use of the whole mind, however briefly, as in samadhi or divine union. The whole mind seems to be one, with no subconscious or superconscious, but with everything open and directed or absorbed, to some degree, in some ultimate wholeness.

It is possible, although uncommon, for one to lose contact with the conscious mind during reflection or contemplation. Reflection is typically characterized by sensory impressions; contemplation, by experiences beyond the senses (supersensory) and beyond reason (intuition). Meditation teachers say, for example, that psychedelic experiences generally seem to involve distortions of normal consciousness, and are often centered in the subconscious dreamworld (including the nightmare realm of the "bad trip"), rather than occurring in the more strictly nonsensory and inspiring world of the superconscious.

All major schools of meditation warn against using meditation to seek to develop psychic abilities. Psychic abilities are not accepted as signs or proof of spiritual growth, but many even indicate a predisposition towards backsliding. Psychic abilities at the personality level are said to lead, if sought after, to increasing self-aggrandizement, unbalanced growth, and the gradual loss of control of spiritual faculties. Neither are psychic abilities to be sought at the superconscious level, for they are described as by-products rather than ends of meditation.

Meditators say, If you get no more out of meditation than learning to concentrate faster and deeper, is this not worthwhile? They claim that meditation teaches one the use of the will, and this leads to knowledge of how to control emotions and mind, which means a steady increase in self-control—and one-pointedness about pursuing one's goal in life. They say it also releases new capacities for love and wisdom, a deeper sense of concern and responsibility, with a concomitant desire to act meaningfully in relation to others.

Ask the average meditator why he meditates and sooner or later he is likely to use the phrase "mind expansion" or "expansion of consciousness." Members of one popular Hindu school (the followers of the Maharishi of the Beatles) like the term "transcendental consciousness."

Consciousness, for meditators, is much more than mere awareness and knowingness. Consciousness is regarded as the irreducible component of life having to do with one's capacity for all conceivable types of present and potential relationships. The expansion of consciousness is the realization of ever more inclusive relationships—of all that goes on within oneself (at the levels, say, of instinct, intellect, and intuition), and how one relates to everything else he is aware of.

Illumination, the experience of Oneness or Unity, is described as a state of being in which all relationships are harmoniously resolved and everything in existence is significantly located within and is a part of an ultimate wholeness. The question, "Who am I?" is said to be resolved in the experience of What one is a vital, meaningful, evolving part of.

What are the characteristics of the superconscious experience? Such scholars as William James, W. T. Stace, Walter N. Pahnke, and many others, categorize the characteristics with such terms as (1) the experience of Oneness or Unity, inwardly and/or outwardly realized; (2) deeply felt positive mood—love and its derivatives; (3) wisdom—intuitive insights; (4)

objectivity and reality—a sense of self-disidentifica-
tion; (5) sense of sacredness; (6) authoritativeness
of the experience; (7) transcendence of time and
space; (8) paradoxicality and ineffability of the experience; (9) awareness of some Other or Being; and
(10) persisting positive changes in one's attitude
and/or behavior.

These "persisting positive changes" are interpreted
as changes towards oneself, others, and life itself. Even
the early stages of meditation are believed to give increasing integration of the personality, new understanding of others and one's responsibility towards
them, and creative and expansive changes in one's
philosophy, values, attitudes, purposes, and behavior.

How to Meditate

"The methods by which we may succeed in eman-
cipating our mind from a self-centered scale of values
are basically the same in all religious faiths," according to Dr. N. Gangulee. "It is interesting to note
the uniformity of the teaching of all religions and
races," Alice A. Bailey observes, "as to the technique
of entrance into the kingdom of the soul. At a certain
point on the path of evolution, it would appear as if
all ways converge and all pilgrims arrive at the same
identical position on the Way. From this point of
junction, they travel the same way, and employ the
same methods, and use a curiously similar phrase-
ology." St. Bernard says, "The words are different,
the paths are many, but one thing is signified: the
paths lead to one Being."

Suppose one wants to learn how to meditate. How
to begin?

The serious way, meditation teachers say, is first
to become familiar with what meditation is. Talk to
people and read books, especially those reflecting

what you consider a wholesome outlook on life. Many resources are available both within and outside of organized religion. Every major religion has an extensive literature of its own. For example, the bibliography in the Rev. Bede Frost's *The Art of Mental Prayer* (London: Society for Promoting Christian Knowledge, 1940) lists over 160 works. The swiftest sampling of other general works might include Lynn J. Radcliff's *Making Prayer Real* (New York: Abingdon Press, 1952); Friedrich Heiler's *Prayer* (New York: Oxford University Press, 1958); Evelyn Underhill's *Worship* (New York: Harper & Brothers, Torchback edition, 1957); Edward Conze's *Buddhist Meditation* (London: George Allen and Unwin Ltd, 1956); and the writings, for example, of Swami Vivekananda on the Hindu yogas and of Daisetz Suzuki on Zen Buddhism.

The Rev. Bede Frost's book is an authoritative introduction to the Ignatian, Franciscan, Carmelite, Salesian, Liguorian, and Oratorian methods of meditation. He points out that St. Ignatius of Loyola, in the 1530's, is generally credited with formalizing the meditative techniques which were to serve as the basis of what is known as the classic method of Christian meditation. Various other forms of meditation exist within the Protestant tradition. For example, Martin Luther, in 1534, developed his own method which is recorded in Rudolph Otto's *Mysticism East and West* (New York: Meridian Books, 1957, a paperback edition of an earlier printing). A well-known brief work in the syncretistic tradition is J. J. Van der Leeuw's *Gods in Exile* (Theosophical Publishing House, Wheaton, Ill., 1959).

The occasional use of an arbitrarily selected meditation form may be diverting, amusing, or even rewarding, the teachers tell us, but add that such meditating in the long-run is worth little. Meditation, they say, should be an integrated part of one's total approach to life. It should be practiced within a compatible, self-developmental psychology, philosophy, or religion. It should be supported by systematic study and by responsible behavior. That is, the Christian should look within his own tradition for a school of meditation that seems suited to him, and the Hindu or Buddhist within his religion, and so on. Various schools of meditation exist outside of organized religion for those who wish "to taste and test" until the right approach is found. For some, the latter approach may center initially on psychological studies of the thinking processes, especially the creative process and intuition, backed by a study of logic, ethics, and general metaphysics.

Meditation teachers seem almost universally agreed that most experiences of the superconscious come first in terms of either love or wisdom or of both simultaneously. The two principal approaches to meditation are based on this recognition. The more common approach is the way of the heart, the path of love, and the other the way of the head, the path of wisdom. Both methods are frequently combined in more advanced or demanding meditation forms. The basic technique, at its simplest, is to think about a symbol or seed-thought, seeking intuitive insight or wisdom, and then to attempt to *experience* or feel its meaning or significance embodied within oneself, "You can think about love," meditation teachers like to say, "But it isn't a concept floating around in the air. You can know it only in yourself as you experience it."

"The best definition of meditation," it has been noted, "is the act of meditating itself." Perhaps the best general understanding of what is involved in the practice of "right meditation"—both its complexity and its promise—may be derived by considering a single meditation form.

Several simple instructions would accompany its experimental use for a few days. "Practice your meditation," a teacher would say, "in a place that affords you solitude and silence. Sit with your spine comfortably erect, forgetting your body, and with closed eyes focused straight ahead. Meditate for about thirty minutes. Use your common sense—avoid the bizarre, maintain calm, stop if you feel any unpleasant physical symptoms such as dizziness or a headache. The good meditation is typically both energizing and inspiring. Act as your 'best self.' Begin your meditation in the consciousness that you, the 'best self,' control your body, emotions, and mind."

The meditation form given is freely adapted from a popular form used in Theravada Buddhism (the Southern School). The standard work of this school on meditation, the *Visuddhimagga,* lists 40 subjects of meditation. Only two of these are considered to be beneficial for anyone at any time: the development of friendliness and the recollection of death. The majority of Buddhist meditations are intended for the use of specific types of people, at particular stages of growth, or for temporary use in dealing with certain problems or developing certain abilities.

This is the Meditation on Unlimited Friendliness

A. With right attitude "Contemplate the dangers of hate and the advantages of forbearance."

B. Develop friendliness towards oneself.

C. Develop friendliness for (a) a spiritual person, (b) a very dear person, (c) an indifferent person, and (d) an enemy.

D. With "evenmindedness" regard oneself and the four persons as alike and equally worthy of unlimited friendliness.

E. Let your sense of friendship gradually embrace the world.

Use of the meditation form would be accompanied by study of the meaning of the terms used, their significance in human relations, and then followed by the effort to practice and experience such unlimited friendliness (with, say, dispassion, discrimination, and detachment) but not in a severe, foolish, or self-denying way.

No meditation form can be said to be typical of other forms. And each, like a gem, requires its own setting. In its proper setting, enhanced by a workable psychology, philosophy, or religion—suitable to oneself and one's own needs—the meditation form becomes a source, if it is maintained, of inexhaustible growth, freedom, and creativity. "Inspired by meditation," an old saying goes, "the meditator himself becomes inspiring."

9.

Gathering In Diffuseness of Thought

MARIE B. BYLES

"Gathering diffuseness of thought" is an expression often used in the Buddhist scriptures. It means pinpointing our usually scattered thoughts, not on anything of this world—not, for instance, on a scientific thesis or musical composition and still less on current gossip—but on what is beyond anything that can be perceived with the five senses or the intellect, which is the sixth sense. The term "beyond" is also taken from the Buddhist scriptures. But Kabir spoke of the "sorrowless land," Christ of the "Kingdom of God," and the Cloud of Unknowing of "that little word God." There are a thousand ways of describing the indescribable.

Gandhi's spiritual son, Vinoba Bhave, said that true Samadhi means perfect equanimity at all times, and Gandhi said that so-called holy men were sometimes rather bad-tempered, i. e., they had not attained Samadhi.

Let us bear all these things in mind as we consider the practice of meditation.

I had been interested in meditation ever since I read Gerald Heard's first booklet on *Training for the Life of the Spirit* about 1942. But in 1957, and during the nine years following, the way opened up to go three times to Burma and twice to Japan, each time for about two months, and join in the meditational practices of these places.

Outside the Burmese Buddhist meditation center of Maha Modhi, near Mandalay,[1] there was a symbol of the Three Limbs of the Perfected Life—Sila (morality or virtue) ; Samadhi (mindfulness, meditation, and concentration) ; and Panna (supreme wisdom). I do not think anyone will quarrel with these three ingredients.

The dominant spirit of Maha Bodhi was that of peace and quietness. There were notices everywhere, "Toe Toe" which meant "shut shut" or "speak very little, speak very quietly, hush-hush." We did not talk as we ate, nor casually if we met. We read nothing, and we had no wirelesses, transistors, or newspapers.

But also there was an atmosphere of enveloping loving-kindness, not only toward the solitary foreigner, but toward all. Everyone was welcomed, whatever his religion. Further, the Instructor's vow was one which precluded teaching for money or fear or for authority of any government, but only for the sake of loving-kindness. I felt I had come home and that the yogis (meditators) were my brothers and sisters. If, therefore, I may seem unduly to favor the type of meditation taught here, it is only fair to remember that what suits one may not suit another, and also that I have not always consistently followed it.

In spite of the silence and loving-kindness, it was an austere monastic regime that we followed.

We spent over twelve hours a day gathering in diffuseness of thought in meditation, and only six in sleeping. We ate no food after lunch at 10 a.m. until 6 a.m. the following day, when we had rice gruel only. Our little meditation huts, many of which were above the water, were without furniture except for bamboo mats on which we sat and slept. We took all the vows of monks—not to kill or injure anything, not to steal or take what was not given, not to be untruthful or indulge in idle gossip, to avoid intoxicants, and to observe chastity, and also the lesser precepts which forbid seeing shows or dancing or listening to music, sleeping on luxurious beds, and self-adornment.

The Instructor was a layman, one of the very few in Burma, where the professional religious is considered the superior. This fact was immensely helpful to me for I have an innate Quakerism which is averse to anyone being considered superior. The Inner Light is within all, and Quakers have no professional clergymen. The Instructor gave me the first initiation ceremony immediately I arrived, and a charming apricot-robed nun, Daw Saranawati, acted as my interpreter. An important aspect of this initiation is the advice that one must not depend upon one's own effort, but merely do the work and leave the result to the Dhamma, remembering "the infinite compassion of the Buddhas." I was bidden to look mentally at the breath coming in and out of the nostrils; that was all, but to note the visions that came and report them to the Instructor. Later, when I did this, he warned me that visions have no importance in themselves—they merely show progress. Too often people take notice of lovely visions and find pleasure in them. To do this is like stopping at a railway station instead of proceeding with the journey. Visions are not real; they do not lead to Nirvana.

Trance state is even more dangerous. Some people have the ability to throw themselves into a trance; others have not. In the early stages it must definitely not be indulged in and, even later, never for pleasure; and it does not lead to Nirvana.

Siddhis, or Iddhis, supernormal powers, may come

as a side line later on. But they, too, must be left behind; they, too, do not lead to Nirvana, nor to Panna.

After about six days some others and I received
a second initiation ceremony, in which we were bidden to change the method and, instead of mentally
looking at the breath, to look mentally at the changing particles of which mind and body are composed,
phyitpyet, (come-go or ceaseless change). In Burma
there are many themes for meditation. The breathing is the most usual; another is the component parts
of the body, the bones and muscles shown on a phy-
siological chart. Our method, the Ledi Sayadaw, is
particularly suitable for Westerners because modern
science shows that all consists of ceaseless change, particles or waves. We were taught to meditate upon
phyit-pyet, and also to repeat this under our breath
whenever we were not meditating, as, for instance,
while we were eating.

At the second initiation ceremony we were bidden
to cease looking at visions and reporting them, and
instead to observe how the body was being affected
and report this. These bodily experiences may come
almost at once and, personally, I thought I had had
enough and to spare already. There is no doubt that
concentration of thought has an extraordinary effect
upon the body. The result may be even vomiting or
dysentery and these effects may remain until the
meditation is lessened or the required lesson is
learned. The Instructor once told us jubilantly that
such-and-such a monk meditator had had eight bowel
movements in one day—very precocious, that monk!
Another thing which the Instructor expected would
come to most of us was "the red hot needles." If anyone sits still and concentrates for even a short time
he can observe little itchings and crawlings which he
probably brushes away unconsciously. We were told
to bear these—they were a good sign—and merely look

at them mentally. In order that these imaginary flies and mosquitoes might not be mistaken for the real thing we were advised to meditate under a mosquito net. These little itchings may later turn into "the red hot needles" which seem to jab at all the tenderest parts of the anatomy. Again we were told to look at them mentally and to bear the pain; they are not real, and before long they will go. They do, fortunately! It is the same with all pain, including boredom. "Never run away from pain; look at it and be one with it," was the sage advice.

Everyone does not suffer similarly when meditating. If the result becomes very serious I question the wisdom of continuing the meditation so intensely, for it seems that the effects can last very long. I am sure that a mere night and morning meditation would never bring about any serious effects.

And now let us remember that meditation alone does not become Samadhi except in so far that it means perfect equanimity at all times. Brother Lawrence was at peace and in the Presence of God as much when he was a cook in the monastery kitchen as when "on his knees at the blessed sacrament." That was perfect Samadhi. Although I thought I had learned to concentrate fairly well I had not attained Samadhi in this sense, for when, at the expiry of a month, I went with Daw Saranawati to the sacred hills of Sagaing, I found I became disturbed over mere trifles. The pendulum had swung too far in concentration; now it swung too far the opposite way.

This does not mean that I decry intensive meditation, although Gandhi never practiced meditation in this manner. Further I wish that we had meditation centers in my country and also meditation instructors. It is obviously easier to learn, say, geology from a human being than from a text book, and the same applies to meditation. But no instructor in meditation should be looked upon as a guru to be obeyed, any more than should a geology lecturer; of course, one follows the teaching with faith, but this is not blind obedience. The only true guru for meditation and for life generally is the Inner Light in our own hearts, and we are all made differently. This is what Gandhi said to Mira Behn, his English disciple:

> This is how I would grow if I were you. But you should grow along your own lines. You will therefore reject all that I have said that does not appeal to your heart and your head. You must retain your individuality at all costs. Resist me when you must. For I may judge you wrongly in spite of all my love for you. I do not want you to impute infallibility to me.[2]

The Burmese Instructor took exactly the same attitude. On my second visit I had a strange urge to go to the meditation center at Mohnyin. He said that he did not understand why but that it was the Dhamma who was leading me. And when I left finally he said, "The Dhamma has brought you here and the Dhamma will be your teacher."

Alas! It would not be easy to find such humble people as the Maha Bodhi Instructor and Mahatma Gandhi.

Without the example of humbleness, the teacher might be a good teacher of the technique of meditation, but he (or she) would not set the example of self-naughting in actual living, and selflessness is the foundation of the road to Nirvana. It is true that each must work through his own individuality, yet this very individuality must be subservient to the direction of the universal whole—one of the paradoxes of life. However, the absence of a human instructor does not preclude the learning of meditation. And with or without a human instructor it seems that the Inner Light usually needs twenty or thirty years of practice before it can bring about fruition.

And now we come to Japan and Zen[3] meditation, the opposite of Burmese vipassana or insight meditation. By and large Buddhist meditation in Burma had no ritual or ceremony attached to it. At Maha Bodhi meditators were asked not even to sing suttras[4] aloud lest they disturb the quiet of others. But in Zen in Japan exact ritual was fundamental.

Zen is popular in the West today, largely, I think, because it goes straight to the essence of all religions without obscure and outmoded symbolism which the modern mind cannot accept and without which people may delude themselves into thinking there is a short cut to enlightenment. To surrender yourself to Christ and to step one foot off the top of a hundred foot pole may mean the same psychological experience but the latter is a preferable symbolism to the modern mind—although not easier to put into practice.

Like most religious faiths, Zen has hardened into outer forms and its meditation demands exact ritual. As I have not a temperament to which ritual appeals I may therefore be unfair in my judgment. But I merely describe what I witnessed.

It was thanks to the Rev. Ruth Fuller Sasaki, a very learned American woman and herself a Zen priest, that I was able to live at a Zen temple in Kyoto and attend Zazen (meditation) in Zendo (meditation hall) built especially for Europeans and without which it would be almost impossible for a European with limited time to see Zen meditation in actual practice.

The Zendo has doors at front and back and two platforms along both sides covered with tatami matting and with a few hard cushions. In monasteries the Zendo is used by the monks for sleeping as well as for meditation. At the rear end there is a shrine

to Manjusri, the god of wisdom, with its back to the
meditators, and his sword, shaped like a small oar,
hangs at the side of the shrine. The presiding priest
offers it to the image of Manjusri, puts it over his
shoulder, and strikes round the Zendo using it to hit
meditators who he thinks will benefit from this and,
as he is now believed to be endowed with the wisdom
of Manjusri, he cannot err. Mrs. Sasaki's Zendo for
Europeans would have been the only one in Japan
where the stick was not used to hit meditators.

Having first removed our shoes and put on slippers
we entered the front door, bowed with hands prayer-
wise, and walked along the edge—it is forbidden to
walk diagonally—to the seat alloted, bowed to our
seat, bowed to the hall, climbed up onto our cushions,
being careful not to touch the edge of the platform,
and sat down lotus-style with buttocks on at least one
low cushion.

O Sho San, the priest, tinkled a cup-shaped bell,
worshipped at Manjusri's shrine, banged the clappers
(so loudly that I nearly jumped out of my skin!) took
down Manjusri's sword, offered it at the shrine, put
it over the shoulder like a gun, and walked sternly
and silently round the dimly lit Zendo while we sat
with eyes half-closed and concentrated on the draw-
ing-in of the breath as we counted mentally to the
number of ten. (Later on, the student would be given
a koan[5] to meditate upon instead of the breathing.)
As the priest went round he corrected any fault in
posture or any tendency to drowsiness—except in
the European Zendo on these occasions he would tap
you on the shoulder with Manjusri's sword, bow to
you, and you would bow in return and lean forward;
he would then whack you on the left side twice (four
times in winter) and similarly on the right side. The
mere fact of being corrected in posture, let alone
whacked, completely prevented any meditation on

my part, more especially during the week of intensive meditation when we could hear the monks in the monastery only a short way off being very frequently whacked. The procedure drew a black impenetrable curtain between the Infinite and me, making impossible the focus of thought on what is Beyond Thought.

At the end of a half an hour there were more clappers and bells and we were given a short interval to relieve aching muscles.

Further clappers and bells ushered in the second half-hour and also ended it. This time we got down from the platform and, hands on stomach, walked briskly round the Zendo inside or out according to the weather. The march ended with the clappers and we resumed our seats.

The third period began and ended like the others with bells and clappers but was followed by a formal tea ceremony, commenced with particularly sharp claps. We changed to kneeling-on-buttocks, took the tea bowl from the rear and placed it on the wooden edge of the platform. The tea officer walked round the Zendo, slipped off his slippers, and lit incense at Manjusri's shrine. As he walked round to fill the tea bowls we each took up our own, bowed to it and held it out, being careful to raise the left hand palm up when he had filled it to our liking. (I once watched him deliberately let a newcomer's bowl overflow because she did not realize the formality necessary.) We then bowed, lifted our bowls, drank, and placed them back at the rear of our seats. The priest completed the ceremony with a few more tinkles, bowing before the shrine and following with more clappers. We then came down from the platform and stretched our limbs.

The fourth period was like the others, but it was ended by our kneeling formal-wise and chanting sutras[4] in Sino-Japanese, which of course no one understood, but which I was told had an inner significance based on years of experience of ancient masters. The sutra chanting was accompanied by tapping on a "wooden fish," a semispherical affair with a large mouth, and also accompanied by tinkling of bells.

This is the procedure followed in the Rinzai Zen Sect. In the Soto Zen Sect meditators sit facing the wall with their backs to the presiding priest carrying and using Manjusri's sword. A nun of that sect described to me a daily life which savored of deliberate sadism.

Once again, let me be fair and say that possibly modern Zen has been the training ground of people who learned to gather in diffuseness of thought and find equanimity. It certainly precludes trance state and the acquirement of supernormal powers. It has been stated to be able to train good soldiers, and that you must be cruel to be kind—two things about the desirability of which there may be a great difference of opinion. And whatever one may think of the use of Manjusri's sword or of deliberately beating people to force them to interview the Roshi or guru, it is a fact that the daily round of living provides Manjusri's sword just as it provides the hair shirt. There is no need for fallible men to be deliberately cruel and it is usually sadistic for them to be so.

As well as practicing Zen meditation in Japan I was privileged there to sit in meditation with two different groups each of which practiced a novel form of breathing. As you drew the breath in you *deflated* the abdomen; as you let it out you *inflated* it; that is the opposite of what comes naturally, but it is fairly easy to get into the rhythm of it. I cannot think, however, that it would be wise for Westerners, because it would not conduce to relaxation, which is, above all, what we require.

And now, if we return to the objective, which is the gathering-in of thought and equanimity at all times, I suggest that the Nembutzu, as it is called in Japan, has importance in meditation. It is the same as the Hindu idea of "doing Japa."

Shinran, who unconsciously founded the Shinshu sect which is based upon the practice of Nembutzu, and his saintly master Honen, of the 12th and 13th centuries, lived in troublous times like our own. Neither had anything against the recognized practices of meditation and good works. But in such difficult times they felt that these were beyond the ability of average people and that there must be an easier way, within reach of everyone, whereby salvation from sorrow might be found. The Pure Land or Judo School turned to the great vow of the Buddha Amida, who refused to enjoy the bliss of Nirvana until he had drawn all beings into that "Pure Land." Honen and Shinran after him found in this what they called "the easy way." All that was necessary was the ceaseless repetition of the words "Buddha Amida Butsu" (adoration to the Buddha of Boundless Light and Love) and faith in his all-redeeming vow. This is the Nembutzu.

The Ittoen Community[6] with which I stayed in Japan on the second visit held Shinran in high esteem, and while I was there I saw the film telling his life story. Although I could not understand the Japanese dialogue, there was no more doubt about the troublous times than about the glorious autumn coloring. There was also no doubt about Shinran's anguish of heart when he found he was not a natural celibate and fell in love. By marrying he departed from the ideal of celibacy we find in India and Burma, but also he showed that a householder's life was no obstacle to finding enlightenment by means of the Nembutzu method.

Of course, we of the self-styled scientific West could not repeat "Buddha Amida Butsu" for the very reason that we have no faith that such a being exists. What we think *does* exist, and perhaps we are the poorer for not having this belief. But it still remains that we do not do so and this must be accepted as fact. There are, however, many other phrases concerning what we *do* believe and these will serve equally well. We believe that the universe is held by perfect law and enfolded in infinite love, and guided by what is not self and which is infinitely kind. The right phrase—mantra—will come to each one who really wants to find it. And then it only remains to repeat this phrase millions of times.

By this means we gather in diffuseness of thought and focus on what is beyond and so find equanimity. The likeness of this to the Hindu "doing Japa" is obvious, or to the Tibetan saying "Om Mani Padme Hum." But also it is no different from the "Phyit-Pyet" we were taught to repeat at the Maha Bodhi Meditation Center, or that "little word of God" advised by the author of *The Cloud of Unknowing*. It was Gandhi's method and he died with the word Rama (God) on his lips. Finally, it can be likened to Coue's[7] way of autosuggestion to bring about physical cures by the patient repetition night and morning, while half-drowsy, the sentence "Every day and in all respects I'm getting better and better." Coue found that if people willed themselves to get better the law of reversed effort came into effect and they became worse. Of our own egotistical efforts and our puny little intellects we can accomplish nothing. But by constant repetition the subconscious mind and the imagination are affected and the result achieved by Shinran's "easy way."

There are three small matters that should be considered whatever the method of meditation adopted.

Should we ever change our mantra? In India and Burma it is usually considered that we should not do so. But a friend and I who discussed it from our own experience found that we each had changed unconsciously as we progressed. We shall be led by the Inner Light to change if a change is wise. So we need not worry.

The next matter is that of posture. In India and Japan straight-sitting is usually considered essential, the lotus-posture for preference; and I should think that a straight back would conduce to proper breathing, and deep breathing would certainly be good for health. But in Burma the male meditators merely sat cross-legged, and the women with both legs to the side, and both tended to slouch—even the statues of the Buddha were often a little round-shouldered. If we are unwell, the only comfortable posture is reclining or lying. At Maha Bodhi we were told we could meditate sitting, standing, lying, or walking and there are many stories showing the Buddha meditating as he walked up and down. Incidentally, if you favor lotus style you will find it more comfortable if a low hard cushion is placed under the buttocks; once you learn to sit that way you will find it the most comfortable of all positions. But do not pretend to yourself that you will learn it merely by sitting that way for an hour night and morning.

The last small matter is that of a rosary, which is in universal use in the East and in Roman Catholicism. Every one is different; all I can say is that I have found that to repeat the mantra to the 108 beads of the Eastern rosary is long enough to gain the necessary relaxation.

But whatever we do or do not do let us always remember that gathering in diffuseness of thought is only one aspect of the perfected life. The Buddha laid down Eight Steps to attain the perfected life, and meditation was only one of them. And no religion has said that meditation alone is necessary. Nor can we forget the Tibetan words of wisdom from the *Voice of Silence:* "Believe thou not that sitting in dark forests in proud seclusion and apart from men . . . will lead thee to the goal of final liberation."

This is not a learned dissertation nor does it profess to examine theories. I am interested only in the practical experience of gathering in diffuseness of thought and finding equanimity. If this helps lead to Moksha, Enlightenment, and Nirvana, well and good. If it does not, let us be content if we find inner peace and a quiet ending when death comes. This is how my Burmese nun friend described the death of one who had practiced meditation at Maha Bodhi:

> Daw Seiktara's mother has died. Her daughter was satisfied for she met a yogi's (meditator's) death. Daw Seiktara chanted suttas[4] and struck the gong-bell rhythmically. Her mother breathed her last silently as the sound waves of the gong-bell slowly died away. When we reach our last moment that is how we too would choose to have our own Phyit-Pyet pass away while we are still mindful.
>
> How beautiful is a yogi's death!

References

1. Byles, M. B. *Journey Into Burmese Silence* and *Paths to Inner Calm* (both Allen & Uuwin)
2. *Bapu's Letter to Mira* p. 31 (Navajivan Publishing House)
3. *Paths to Inner Calm*
4. Sutta (Pali), Sutra (Sanscrit) a sacred chant.
5. Koan: A kind of nonsense saying whose object is to tease the intellect until it admits defeat thereby allowing of an understanding beyond intellect.
6. Ittoen Community - see Tenkl *San A New Road to Ancient Truth* (Allen & Unwin)
7. Baudouin, C. *Suggestion and Autosuggestion* (Allen & Unwin)

10.

Meditation and Way of Life

The philosophy of the East, in which the present-
day youth of the West especially shows a keen interest, lays great emphasis on the inner and deeper
aspects of life—the life of the spirit—in contrast to
materialistic and surface values. It emphasizes that
everything in the universe, including man, is a frag-
ment of the One Supreme Principle and that the purpose of life for man is to realize this as a living truth—
what is so very beautifully, and yet simply, described
by Samkaracharya as *Tat tvam asi, or* "That am I."

An ancient approach in the East to a conscious
realization of this truth has been through yoga. As
a philosophy it deals with the profound truths per-
taining to man, life, and the universe. It has around
it an atmosphere of mystery, in the sense that beyond
certain depths it is more a state of experiencing. At
the same time, the technique of yoga enables one to
experience the mystery of all mysteries within oneself.
A yogi is one who discovers within himself his oneness with all beings, when his consciousness functions
in unison with the One Consciousness, when "he can
contemplate the inner heavens in the daylight of waking life."

Meditation is the technique of exploring the inner space of man, a space which, if fathomed, can lead him to the center of his very being. Although labeled a technique, it is not a mechanical or technological process such as probing into outer space. Nor is it a becoming something, though often a goal is referred to. It is more a process which takes place when the mind begins to see and comprehend things and situations as they truly are. It is said that the Buddha, while he struggled by self-denial and extreme asceticism to find something, realized that he was advancing nowhere. But the moment he let go all ambitions to reach a goal and recognized that there was nothing to achieve, that very night he attained the state of Sambodhi (the Fully Awakened state), the step toward complete enlightenment. Neither is meditation an escape from life. It is very much linked with life in the sense that the ground covered at every stage is dependent on one's attitude to life, the way the problems of life, with its apparent pairs of opposites, are encountered.

While the extreme interest in meditation, particularly in the West, is to be welcomed, there is danger that its wide popularity, and increasing familiarity with it, may reduce it to a purely mechanical, even a commercialized process, with "instant methods" of reaching states of yoga. It is regretted that there are self-styled "yogis" who proliferate and thrive on such ignorance.

Meditation also, unfortunately, is associated with the awakening of one's psychic faculties, such as seeing visions, astral projections, hearing sounds, and the like. In the East, even ecstatic experiences are sometimes associated with the awakening of one's lower faculties. The effects of LSD and similar drugs, which are psychic in nature, are often confused with the awakening of spiritual potencies. The influences of

the drugs range from psychedelic effects to an experience of a certain ecstasy. While under the influence
of such a drug, one may get a glimpse of another
world than the physical (if one needs such proof),
but this can never be a substitute for, or a way to, the
Path of Liberation. As John Blofeld points out in
The Way of the Power (p. 33), ". . . bliss so easily
attainable would be likely to reconcile them to life
as it is and induce them to be content with drug-
induced experiences instead of actually treading the
path." Surely, looking at a picture of the canyon can
never be a substitute for the breathless beauty and
awesomeness of which one is aware when beholding
it face to face.

The acquirement or exercise of such powers, even
of a high order, tends to distract the mind from a true
perspective and may lead to unforeseen temptations
and pitfalls. It is only when one has completely sub-
limated one's lower nature—the still lurking animalis-
tic passions and lusts—and acquired true *vairagya*
(detachment) that one is cable of coping with such
powers and utilizing them for beneficent purposes.
This is corroborated by Patanjali in the *Yoga-sutras*.
Meditation was never intended primarily for the
acquirement of *siddhis*. To begin with, it is to cleanse
the mind and heart of all disturbing influences, to
sweep away the "sediments" clouding the vision.

The *Dhammapada* (one of the miscellaneous works
of the *Sutta-Pitaka* or Discourses of the Buddha) begins with these striking words: "Mind precedes
things, dominates them, creates them." "All that we
are is the result of what we have thought. We are
founded and built upon our thoughts." What we are
now is as we have thought in the past. What we
think now, we become. So it is said that "[if] mind is
comprehended, all things are comprehended." (*Rat-
na-megha-sutta*) An understanding of the mind with

the complexities into which it has evolved leads to an understanding of oneself.

The *Dhammapada* speaks also of the "taming of the mind," as this brings happiness in the true sense. It states further that if a man does not know the true law, if his mind is troubled, his knowledge (meaning wisdom) can never be perfect. The chapter on mind ends with these signifcant words: "A well-directed mind will do us greater service."

The many ills of man arise from the state of his mind and can be traced to the psychological complexes built in its framework—complexes born out of pressures and imbalances in his environment, and more truly in himself. In such a state the life energy, instead of being a free flow from within outward, becomes stagnant or only dribbles through. Man is intended to let the life within express itself through his thoughts, feelings, actions. If the flow is smooth, regular, without impediments, there is a maximum expression of the energy in its innate purity and color. The greatest barrier to such a free flow is the mind with all its modifications.

Meditation is the process by which the mind is emptied of its contents—the barriers and not the factual data—and the way is cleared for the full expression of the life-energy. The very first step in this process is concentration, which is generally understood as fixing the mind on an object or thought. In *Vimuttimagga (The Path of Freedom,* p. 39) it is said that "Concentration means that one has purity of mind, endeavors steadfastly, dwells with the truth having the benefit of tranquility and is not distracted." It is interesting here to note that the process of concentration, besides focusing the attention steadfastly without any distraction, is also associated with purity and tranquility of mind. It is only logical that steadfast attention can arise only out of a state of purity and tranquility, and when concentration is understood not as hypnotic suggestion, not as a mechanized process, but as a state of mind intimately related to one's life. It implies a state of mind not bound or pulled in diverse directions by *kama*. It is a mind which is not subject to *tanha* (thirst). As explained further in the same text, it is "not allowing one's mind to be bent by the strong wind of passion." (p. 39)

The *Abhidhamma* defines concentration as "What fixes the mind aright, causes it to be not dependent on any, causes it to be unmoved, undisturbed, tranquilized and non-attached . . ." The function, manifestation and cause of concentration, are explained in the *Vimuttimagga* (p. 39) : "Overcoming of hatred is its function; tranquility is its manifestation; non-association with defilement and the mind obtaining freedom are its near cause." The text further states that "He who maintains the mind and its mental properties in a state of equilibrium" is the one who can successfully observe concentration. The *Bhaga-vad-gita* describes in similar words one who is stable of mind. When Arjuna puts the question, "What is the mark of him who is stable of mind, steadfast in contemplation?" Sri Krishna (besides mentioning other qualifications) says, "He whose mind is free from anxiety amid pains, indifferent amid pleasures, loosed from passion, fear and anger." (2.54,56) In other words, one who is balanced alike to pleasure and pain, one who has the spirit of renunciation in him can concentrate in the true sense.

Although all these qualifications point to an advanced stage of concentration, the texts are quite explicit that concentration, the first step to *dhyana*, cannot be brought about merely by a mechanical process. To concentrate is to reach a state of purity of mind, and attaining that state of concentration is intimately linked to the way of living. The less one's life is swayed by turbulent passions, the easier one can reach this state, and the greater is his fixity of purpose. It is a familiar experience that when one is subject to strong emotions—grief, joy, jealousy, etc.—even outward concentration on one's work is well-nigh impossible. The *Vimuttimagga* lists the obstacles to concentration as "lust, hatred, indolence, rigidity, agitation, uncertainty, delusion, absence of joy and bliss." The factors that promote concentration are "renunciation, non-hatred, non-disturbances, brightness." Renunciation is to be understood not as a running away from life but rather what the *Bhagavad-Gita* describes as doing one's *dharma* with an utter detachment so far as results are concerned.

The practice of meditation is considered by many as "the yoga par excellence" and so they resort to it without certain basic minimum qualifications. The *Bhagavad-Gita* considers as prerequisite for meditation a life free of selfish aims, where desire for personal enjoyment and gratification has no place, and where one's life is free from all fear and anger. Here the meditation referred to is that in which one deliberately sets out to span the bridge between what one truly is and what one appears to be, and to scale the heights to the One Consciousness. Such a meditation, without the necessary qualifications, can only lead to "dangerous mediumistic psychisms or neurotic dissociations of the personality." But the meditation reflecting on the eternal truths, or directed toward the Supreme, does not involve any strenuous concentration and can be undertaken by everyone at all stages of the Path.

The *Vimuttimagga* gives the requisites for concentration as virtue, contentment, shielding of the faculties, moderation on food, and being intent on wisdom. The preparatory qualifications mentioned in the *Yoga-sutras* are very similar: austerity, self-study, forgetting of one's self, self-restraint, non-violence born out of a recognition of the underlying unity of all life, truthfulness, abstaining from all misappropriation, non-possessiveness, purity and contentment.

So it is very apparent that concentration in a deeper sense is a striving toward purity of mind, freeing it from moving along set grooves and patterns. For the very same reason it cannot be freed by a mere technique. In *Anguttara Nikaya* there is a statement:

> Whatsoever there is of evil, connected with evil, belonging to evil—all issues from the mind.
> Whatsoever there is of good, connected with good, belonging to good—all issues from the mind.

And it can be added that whatever the mind is, is only a reflection of what one is, the kind of life one leads, and one's relationships with others. Also, whatever one is in the mind is reflected in one's actions and feelings, and a change within will necessarily bring about an outer change.

Manas, which is a better word for mind, connoting all its aspects, is in essence part of the primordial consciousness, stemming from *Mahat* (Universal Mind). Liberation can come only by restoring it to its original state so that one can look into it as in a mirror. Such a state cannot be induced from without.

The meditation is to be such that it gives a certain mental stance to face the various problems of life. However small may be the ground cleared, it has to be something which can bring about a change in ourselves—a change which can retune our thought and feeling relationship. Man needs to know not only the meaning of life but also what life expects from him as a human being—and life embraces his relationship with things and environment, with the outer and inner man.

Buddhism speaks of building virtues as one of the stages of meditation. And the *Abhidhamma* defines virtue as "destruction of sense-desires by renunciation." Man's life is dominated, subtly or openly, by the quality of lust for power and the fear that he may lose it. All problems can be eventually traced to these factors. So, by a state of detachment within, one can free oneself from these two dominant qualities and then the many-faceted virtue of love and compassion for all beings blossoms from within.

In Buddhism, especially in the original teachings of the Buddha, can be found a variety of methods of "mind training" or meditation by which the mind regains its original quality. All these ways eventually lead to the central theme of "Mindfulness" which is sometimes spoken of as "the heart of Buddhist meditation." The *Satipatthana-Sutta* (in the *Majjhima-* and *Digha-Nikaya* of the *Sutta Pitaka*) describes in great detail this way of Mindfulness. It is said that among the Buddhists no other discourse is so highly venerated as this Sutta. This is one of the very few discourses which the Buddha "himself marked out by introducing and concluding them in a particularly emphatic and solemn way." (*The Heart of Buddhist Meditation,* p. 12) This and the singular effect of its practice explains its wide adoption by the Buddhists. The methods of Zen meditation can be traced to the "Way of Mindfulness."

The method starts with training the mind to face the day-to-day problems in their true perspective, as Right Mindfulness is the basis for Right Living and Right Thinking. What is Mindfulness? Though the terms "technique" and "training" are used, it is to be understood that it is not a mechanized process divorced from living. Neither is it a mystical state. It is just pure and simple attention to all objects and persons, to what one does, including one's bodily movements. Buddhism speaks of different types of Mindfulness: Mindfulness of Breathing, Mindfulness of Posture, Mindfulness of Feeling, and so on. But in every case the technique is associated with a coordination of one's way of life and the spiritual practice. It is considered that "even the most ordinary activity in its own way, should be utilized for the work of Liberation." (*The Heart of Buddhist Meditation*, p. 54) As is pointed out in the Tibetan wisdom, "an art of living which will enable one to utilize each activity as an aid on the Path" is indispensable to meditation.

Buddha's system of meditation, *Satipatthana,* is an art of living. Whatever type of Mindfulness is chosen, in each case the technique starts with the outer physical observance and gradually proceeds to comprise the entire man and his field of experience. For instance, the Mindfulness of Breathing starts with bare observation of the natural flow of breath, with a steady attention, with no strain or rigidity. As a regular practice this results in equalizing and calming the smooth flow of breath. Later still it leads to a tranquilization and deepening of the entire life-rhythm. The final outcome of Mindfulness of Breathing is to lead one to a development of insight. It starts with quietening all irritations and refining the sensitiveness of the mind. Gradually the receptivity and reflective capacity increases and the reactions to things and situations are slowed down.

Mindfulness of Posture is aimed to bring about a critical awareness of the impersonal nature of the body and create in the practitioner a feeling of detachment from the body. Different forms of Mindfulness are indicated to suit the requirement of each individual. A sensual person is advised to practice Mindfulness of the Body, to think of the body as a conglomeration of cells, blood, flesh, etc., resulting in non-sensuality. Mindfulness in one's daily activities lends a quality of improvement to the manner of performance, a keener perception and awareness of things and situations. Even the insignificant commonplace things begin to reveal depths of beauty and wisdom. The mind gets "uncompounded," life acquires simplicity with an inherent beauty. Life becomes more and more a "direct experiencing," the mainsprings of true knowledge are deepened, and true comprehension becomes possible. Meditation related to the way of living as an all-round Mindfulness results in accepting oneself as one is, in bringing about a harmony between the inner "I" and the outer "I".

The gap between the life one actually lives and the spiritual practice one attempts gradually narrows and the domain of meditation and living merges. Meditation as Mindfulness becomes "an incessant inner soliloquy" freeing the mind from all patterns of behavior and dissolving all conflicts. One begins to touch the "well-ordered center" in oneself wherein is one's true being. The life energy flows from within outward uninterruptedly, smoothly, and there is reflected in one's thinking, feelings, and actions a genuine concern for another's well-being, a deep compassion for another's suffering, and a true brotherly love. The "Song of Life" is once again heard.

11.

Christian Mysticism

EDITH SCHLOSSER

It is an ironic fact that, despite its development of the materialistic sciences, the Western world has determinedly ignored the existence of a wider science that has a history extending back thousands of years. Now that it has been proved, to the satisfaction of most modern scientists, that matter resolves itself into energy, the basis of scientific materialism is being called into question. Science now accepts, as a legitimate interest, man's *consciousness*. An awareness that consciousness, as well as form, is evolving has long been the basis for man's practice of meditation.

Therefore, it is not surprising that many people today are seeking for answers not supplied by science about this inner state. The Christian religion, perhaps because its orthodoxy has also largely ignored the ancient wisdom, has failed the esoteric seekers in general, which is why modern youth has been turning to the oriental religions and philosophies for something missing in their own culture. Among other things, they have turned to yoga and to the practice of meditation, using the techniques that have been recorded from time immemorial.

It is a second ironic fact that these techniques are not really strangers to our Christian religion. Some mystics have recorded their experiences and the techniques. It is therefore possible to discover that they were using the same techniques as do the yogis and others who gain enlightenment. All seekers have followed the path approved by their own religion—the goal was ever the same. Many modern Christians, aware of the need to return to the hidden wisdom, are not abandoning their childhood faith, but are exploring it in depth and practicing meditation along Christian lines. It is impossible for any orthodoxy to eradicate the ancient wisdom.

An examination of the writings of the mystics shows how men and women have experienced exactly what has been presented as the goal of yoga: union with the divinity within, the God immanent.

The studies that have been made comparing the techniques described by Christian mystics with those recommended in other religions reveal the universality of method, regardless of the path. And the great Christian saints, poets, and philosophers have known the truth of the Christ within! Christianity has failed generally to teach the techniques, and it is for these that many have turned to any available books from other sources. Unfortunately, the one thing the books cannot give is a shot of *intensity,* so that many practice techniques indifferent to this major inner requirement. This has led to some criticism from those who say there is a lot of talking about it, a lot of concentration on methods, but there is a missing ingredient. Dr. I. K. Taimni has reminded us in his *Gayatri*. ch. v, that "there are a large number of people who allow themselves to be lulled into spiritual sleep by brilliant expositions of philosophical doctrines by intellectually clever people, and who wake up too late in life to find that their theoretical study is not the slightest use to them in solving life's problems or in gaining any measure of inner peace."

However, some who make this criticism are creating pitfalls for themselves, then discovering how difficult is the path and how easy it is to be lulled into byways instead of following the path.

The first step in meditation is right intention, which includes a strength of application not easily achieved. On this, the mystic John Ruysbroeck has written, in an Essay on Simplicity of Intention, in *Flowers of a Mystic Garden*: "In every action of our lives we must hold to this simplicity . . . . It is the single eye . . . . It is this simplicity which will, at the last, offer to God our whole vital activity."

This simplicity of intention is to be fortified by love. This is what our young people are often stressing. Ruysbroeck puts it this way: "The intelligence shall know God in its light; love shall enjoy God without intermediary."

Juliana of Norwich and Ramon Lull can be quoted on this topic. Juliana's often-quoted phrase is: "Wouldst thou wit thy lord's meaning in this thing? Wit it well. Love was His meaning. Who shewed it thee? Love. Wherefore shewed He it thee? For love." (*Revelations of Divine Love*)

Ramon Lull, in *The Book of the Lover and the Beloved*, recorded his "mystic converse with the All-Powerful" and wrote: "What meanst thou by Love? said the Beloved. It is to bear on one's heart the sacred marks and the sweet words of the Beloved. It is the desire for 'the above all things.'" Extravagant phrases, but indicative of the complete abandonment of all desires save the one. And without quoting Brother Lawrence, it seems timely to refer to his constancy of meditative thought on love and his intent to make every act, however menial, an expression of love.

Detachment is another goal for those engaging in meditation. This was the subject of a sermon given by Meister Eckhart, the mystic who did not spare words to describe his experiences. He admits to reading "heathen philosophers and sages" in his search for "the best and highest virtue whereby a man may knit himself most narrowly to God" and concludes that "It is none other than absolute detachment from all creatures." In another place we find the phrase, "to be empty of creatures is to be full of God, and to be full of creatures is to be empty of God." He uses the words "crowd" and "creatures" to mean activities of the mind. "If you are to experience this noble birth [of the Christ within] you must depart from all crowds. The crowds are the agents and their activities: memory, understanding and will in all their diversification. You must leave them all; sense perception, imagination and all that you discover in self or intend to." Does this remind us somewhat of Krishnamurti?

The problem in Christianity has been that of reconciling the teaching of the Trinity, including Jesus as the Son, with the teaching of God immanent and the Christ as the divine spark within all men. It is interesting to read how early scholars who were inclined toward mysticism tried to reconcile their personal discoveries with Church doctrine.

Meister Eckhart struggled with this problem in many of his sermons. He described "the apex of the soul" as "a barren wilderness, barren Godhead, negative divine." If only he could have safely used the ancient gnostic teachings, how much easier it would have been! We think of the "not this, not that" of Hindu teachings relating to the Absolute. One of the best and most concise books on the subject is *The Teachings of the Mystics* by Walter R. Stace, in which Meister Eckhart's descriptions of this "apex of the soul" and "the birth of Christ" which takes place in it have been extracted from his sermons for our

convenient use. Stace makes it clear that this is identical with the Self of the Upanishads and the Mind-
Essence in the Buddhist book, *The Awakening of
Faith*. His extracts are so selected that it becomes
obvious that meditation as practiced by Christian
mystics is the same as that of all others seeking union
with the divine Self. It is the discipline we are still
urged to practice—the concentration, right use of
imagination, detachment, leading to the higher discipline of contemplation. We, too, know the difficulty
of this last hurdle, the momentary glimpse of the
Real, the problem of being constantly drawn back
by our own attachments to the illusory world of the
personal self.

A book report by Robert Kirsch in the *Los Angeles
Times* of September 8, 1970, cited the Italian critic,
Cesare Pavese, as saying, "The surest and quickest
way for us to arouse the sense of wonder is to stare,
unafraid, at a single object. Suddenly—miraculously—
it will look like something we have never seen before." This describes exactly one of the early steps
in meditation, so it is interesting to compare it with
Eckhart's words: "The soul gets at things by means
of ideas and the idea is an entity created by the soul's
agents. Be it a stone or a rose or a person or whatever it is that is to be known, first an idea is taken
and then absorbed, and in this way the soul connects
with the phenomenal world." This taking of an object and seeing it differently can certainly lead to
some deeper understanding of the true nature of
matter.

It is interesting in these days of drug-culture to
read the warnings given about visions. The writings
of St. John of the Cross are seeded with warnings
about mistaking visions for reality. While still a
young man, he worked closely with St. Teresa of
Avila, whose rapturous descriptions of her visions in-

dicate her intensely emotional nature. Her Lord visited her, spoke with her, and seems to have somewhat embarrassed her by appearing at the most inconvenient times, according to her autobiography. St. Teresa and St. John were both members of the Carmelite order, and were making efforts toward reform, which got them into considerable trouble with the higher powers. St. John was imprisoned for, and his life greatly endangered by, his activities. The point for present consideration, however, is that with his help, St. Teresa learned to distinguish between the visions and the final goal, which she seems to have reached. For once her description is terse, for when she says she has reached the highest point, she adds: "By highest point I mean when the faculties are lost through being closely united with God." She advises her reader that he will recognize that point, for "he will neither see, nor hear, nor perceive." But, she adds, "This complete transformation of the soul in God lasts but a short time and it is only while it lasts that none of the soul's faculties is able to perceive or know what is taking place."

St. John of the Cross, whose phrase "dark night of the soul" is familiar to most Christians, calls meditation "a discursive mental activity by means of images, forms and figures that are produced imaginatively . . . as happens, for example, when we picture in our imagination Christ crucified." But he adds, "The soul must be emptied of all these imagined forms, figures and images, and it must remain in darkness in respect to these internal senses if it is to attain Divine union."

This is clearly in line with the teaching of ancients that the visions are still in the illusory world; the Reality is beyond and involves plunging into the silence or darkness beyond the mental world. St. John wrote, "Though in darkness the soul walks securely"—a beautiful phrase. Although the safety of the ladder of the intellect has finally been abandoned, the soul walks in the security of eternal Love.

Today we are in a new age for Christianity. A book recently published by the Theosophical Publishing House, Wheaton, *A Rebirth for Christianity* by Alvin Boyd Kuhn, is a good source for information on how Christianity was deprived of its rightful heritage, the ancient wisdom of the world. Sometimes stern in his denunciation of "two thousand years of a literal reading of the cryptograms of arcane wisdom," Kuhn is nevertheless aware of the transition now in progress, which could "push the human mind far ahead in its progress toward illumination." Priests and nuns are breaking away from the bondage of dogma, and young people are seeking freer air, turning again to the hidden truths. Christianity is in jeopardy only if it refuses to take a new look at its esoteric meaning and fails to allow a new independence for the individual seeking his own Selfhood.

The rebirth has started in such men as Pierre Teilhard de Chardin. He knew the need to develop a Christianity suitable for modern man. He was like the bird that could not be free while held by even the smallest thread. The invisible thread holding Teilhard was his vow of obedience as a Jesuit; it prevented him from soaring as high as his wings would otherwise have taken him. In his *Divine Milieu* he wrote: "Nothing is more consistent or more fleeting—more fused with things or at the same time more separable from them—than a ray of light. If the divine milieu reveals itself to us as an incandescence of the inward layers of being, who is to guarantee us the persistence of this vision? None other than the Ray of Light itself. The diaphany. No power in the world can prevent us from savoring its joys because it happens at a level deeper than any power, and no power in the world—for the same reason—can compel it to appear." Despite his efforts at allegiance, this writer traveled the solitary path through meditation and reached peaks of understanding beyond the heights to which most of us have climbed so far.

There are other modern figures struggling to change the tide. The Theosophical Society has been in the vanguard of progress toward restoration of the occult wisdom, and many of its leaders have been Christian, yet free of bondage to dogma. Annie Besant rebelled against orthodoxy, became atheist, then found in *The Secret Doctrine* the key to real Christianity, and her faith was restored. C. W. Leadbeater, Geoffrey Hodson, and Clara Codd have contributed to the spread of theosophical teachings without disclaiming Christianity. There are others who know the beauty of truth in all religions and dream of closer relationship between world faiths. They know that the Master-teachers have used these faiths as chalices for the precious wisdom in differing world cultures. Theosophy is a unifying force, not a separative teaching. Meditation has been the topic of many theosophical books and, in reading them, we become aware that it can be a universal experience; the discipline and techniques are applicable everywhere because they are a part of a science of human evolutionary development of consciousness. Whether a man be Hindu, Buddhist, Christian, or even agnostic, if he begins with right intention and love he can use his intellect to start toward the right use of knowledge, thus opening the intuition until he rises above the polluted air of prejudicial dogma into the clear atmosphere where those who have traveled separate roads meet in perfect unity and love.

12.

Meditation

CHÖGYAM TRUNGPA

Meditation is a vast subject and there have been many developments throughout the ages and many variations among the different religious traditions. But broadly speaking the basic character of meditation takes on one of two forms. The first stems from the teachings which are concerned with the discovery of the nature of existence; the second concerns communication with the external or universal concept of God. In either case meditation is the only way to put the teachings into practice.

Where there is the concept of an external, "higher" Being, there is also an internal personality—which is known as 'I' or the Ego. In this case meditation practice becomes a way of developing communication with an external Being. This means that one feels oneself to be inferior and one is trying to contact something higher, greater. Such meditation is based on devotion. This is basically an inward, or introvert practice of meditation, which is well known in the Hindu teachings, where the emphasis is on going into the inward state of samadhi, into the depths of the heart. One finds a similar technique practiced in the orthodox teachings of Christianity, where the prayer of the heart is used and concentration on the heart is emphasized. This is a means of

identifying oneself with an external Being and neces-
sitates purifying oneself. The basic belief is that
one is separate from God, but there is still a link,
one is still part of God. This confusion sometimes
arises, and in order to clarify it one has to work
inwards and try to raise the standard of individuality to the level of higher consciousness. This approach makes use of emotions and devotional practices which are aimed at making contact with God
or gods or some particular saint. These devotional
practices may also include the recitation of mantra.

The other principal form of meditation is almost
entirely opposite in its approach, though finally it
might lead to the same results. Here there is no
belief in higher and lower; the idea of different levels,
or of being in an underdeveloped state does not
arise. One does not feel inferior, and what one is
trying to achieve is not something higher than oneself. Therefore the practice of meditation does not
require an inward concentration on the heart. There
is no centralizing concept at all. Even such practices
as concentrating on the chakras, or psychic centres
of the body, are approached in a different way. Although in certain teachings of Buddhism the concept of chakras is mentioned, the practices connected
with them are not based on the development of an
inward centre. So this basic form of meditation is
concerned with trying to see what is. There are
many variations on the form of meditation, but they
are generally based on various techniques for opening oneself. The achievement of this kind of meditation is not, therefore, the result of some long-
term, arduous practice through which we build ourselves up into a "higher" state, nor does it necessitate
going into any kind of inner trance state. It is rather
what one might call 'working meditation' or extro-
vert meditation, where skillful means and wisdom

must be combined like the two wings of a bird. This is not a question of trying to retreat from the world. In fact without the external world, the world of apparent phenomena, meditation would be almost impossible to practice, for the individual and the external world are not separate, but merely co-exist together. Therefore the concept of trying to communicate and trying to become one with some higher Being does not arise.

In this kind of meditation practice the concept of *nowness* plays a very important part. In fact, it is the essence of meditation. Whatever one does, whatever one tries to practice, is not aimed at achieving a higher state or at following some theory or ideal, but simply, without any object or ambition, trying to see what is here and now. One has to become aware of the present moment through such means as concentrating on the breathing, a practice which has been developed in the Buddhist tradition. This is based on developing the knowledge of nowness, for each respiration is unique, it is an expression of *now*. Each breath is separate from the next and is fully seen and fully felt, not in a visualized form, nor simply as an aid to concentration, but it should be fully and properly dealt with. Just as a very hungry man, when he is eating, is not even conscious that he is eating food. He is so engrossed in the food that he completely identifies himself with what he is doing and almost becomes one with the taste and enjoyment of it. Similarly with the breathing, the whole idea is to try and see through that very moment in time. So in this case the concept of trying to become something higher does not arise at all, and opinions do not have much importance. In a sense opinions provide a way to escape; they create a kind of slothfulness and obscure one's clarity of vision. The clarity of our consciousness is veiled by prefabricated concepts and whatever we see we try to fit into some pigeon-hole or in some way make it fit in with our preconceived ideas. So concepts and theories—and, for that matter, theology—can become obstacles. One might ask, therefore, what is the point of studying Buddhist philosophy? Since there are scriptures and texts and there is surely some philosophy to believe in, wouldn't that also be a concept? Well, that depends on the individual, but basically it is not so. From the start one tries to transcend concepts, and one tries, perhaps in a very critical way, to find out what *is*. One has to develop a critical mind which will stimulate intelligence. This may at first cause one to reject what is said by teachers or what is written in books, but then gradually one begins to feel something and to find something for oneself. That is what is known as the meeting of imagination and reality, where the feeling of certain words and concepts meets with intuitive knowledge, perhaps in a rather vague and imprecise way. One may be uncertain whether what one is learning is right or not, but there is a general feeling that one is about to discover something. One cannot really start by being perfect, but one must start with something. And if one cultivates this intelligent, intuitive insight, then gradually, stage by stage, the real intuitive feeling develops and the imaginary or hallucinatory element is gradually clarified and eventually dies out. Finally that vague feeling of discovery becomes very clear, so that almost no doubt remains. Even at this stage it is possible that one may be unable to explain one's discovery verbally or write it down exactly on paper, and in fact if one tried to do so it would be limiting one's scope and would be rather dangerous. Nevertheless, as this feeling grows and develops one finally attains direct knowledge, rather than achieving something which is separate from oneself. As in the analogy of the hungry man, you become one with the subject. This can only be achieved through the practice of meditation. Therefore meditation is very much a matter of exercise— it is a working practice. It is not a question of going into some inward depth, but of widening and expanding outwards.

These are the basic differences between the two types of meditation practice. The first may be more suitable for some people and the second may be more suitable for others. It is not a question of one being superior or more accurate than the other. But for any form of meditation one must first overcome that great feeling of demand and ambition which acts as a major obstacle. Making demands on a person, such as a Guru, or having the ambition to achieve something out of what one is doing, arises out of a built-up desire or wantingness; and that wantingness is a centralized notion. This centralized notion is basically blind. It is like having only one eye, and that one eye being situated in the chest. When you try to walk you cannot turn your head round and you can only see a limited area. Because you can see in only one direction the intelligence of turning the head is lacking. Therefore there is a great danger of falling. This wantingness acts as a veil and becomes an obstacle to the discovery of the moment of nowness, because the wanting is based either on the future or on trying to continue something which existed in the past, so the nowness is completely forgotten. There may be a certain effort to focus on the nowness, but perhaps only twenty per cent of the consciousness is based on the present and the rest is scattered into the past or the future. Therefore there is not enough force to see directly what is there.

Here, too, the teaching of selflessness plays a very

important part. This is not merely a question of denying the existence of Ego, for Ego is something relative. Where there is an external person, a higher Being, or the concept of something which is separate from oneself, then we tend to think that because there is something outside there must be something here as well. The external phenomenon sometimes becomes such an overwhelming thing and seems to have all sorts of seductive or aggressive qualities, so we erect a kind of defense mechanism against it, failing to see that that is itself a continuity of the external thing. We try to segregate ourselves from the external, and this creates a kind of gigantic bubble in us which consists of nothing but air and water or, in this case, fear and the reflection of the external thing. So this huge bubble prevents any fresh air from coming in, and that is "I"—the Ego. So in that sense there is the existence of Ego, but it is in fact illusory. Having established that, one generally wants to create some external idol or refuge. Subconsciously one knows that this "I" is only a bubble and it could burst at any moment, so one tries to protect it as much as one can—either consciously or subconsciously. In fact we have achieved such skill at protecting this Ego that we have managed to preserve it for hundreds of years. It is as though a person has a very precious pair of spectacles which he puts in a box or various containers in order to keep it safe, so that even if other things are broken this would be preserved. He may feel that other things could bear hardship, but he knows that this could not, so this would last longer. In the same way, Ego lasts longer just because one feels it could burst at any time. There is fear of it being destroyed because that would be too much, one would feel too exposed. And there is such character, such a fascinating pattern established outside us, although it is in fact our own reflection. That is why the concept of Egolessness is not really a question of whether there is a Self or not, or, for that matter, whether there is the existence of God or not; it is rather the taking away of that concept of the bubble. Having done so, one doesn't have to deliberately destroy the Ego or deliberately condemn God. And when that barrier is removed one can expand and swim through straight away. But this can only be achieved through the practice of meditation, which must be approached in a very practical and simple way. Then the mystical experience of joy or grace, or whatever it might be, can be found in every object. That is what one tries to achieve through Vipassana, or "Insight" meditation practice. Once we have established a basic pattern of discipline and we have developed a regular way of dealing with the situation—whether it is breathing or walking or what-have-you—then at some stage the technique gradually dies out. Reality gradually expands so that we do not have to use the technique at all. And in this case one does not have to concentrate inwards, but one can expand outwards more and more. And the more one expands, the closer one gets to the realization of centerless existence.

This is the basic pattern of this kind of meditation, which is based on three fundamental factors: firstly, not centralizing inwards; secondly, not having any longing to become higher; and thirdly, becoming completely identified with here and now. These three elements run right through the practice of meditation, from the beginning up to the moment of realization.

Q. You mentioned nowness in your talk, and I was wondering how it is possible to become aware of the absolute through awareness of a relative moment in time?

A. Well, we have to start by working through the

relative aspect, until finally this nowness takes on such a living quality that it is no longer dependent on a relative way of expressing nowness. One might say that *now* exists all the time, beyond the concept of relativity. But since all concepts are based on the idea of relativity, it is impossible to find any words which go beyond that. So nowness is the only way to see directly. First it is between the past and the future—now. Then gradually one discovers that nowness is not dependent on relativity at all. One discovers that the past does not exist, the future does not exist, and everything happens now. Similarly, in order to express space one might have first to create a vase, and then one has to break it, and then one sees that the emptiness in the vase is the same as the emptiness outside. That is the whole meaning of technique. At first that nowness is, in a sense, not perfect. Or one might even say that the meditation is not perfect, it is a purely man-made practice. One sits and tries to be still and concentrates on the breathing, and so on. But then, having started in that way, one gradually discovers something more than that. So the effort one has put into it—into the discovery of nowness, for example—would not be wasted, though at the same time one might see that it was rather foolish. But that is the only way to start.

Q. For meditation, would a student have to rid himself of Ego before he started, or would this come naturally as he is studying?

A. This comes naturally, because you can't start without Ego. And basically Ego isn't bad. Good and bad doesn't really exist anywhere, it is only a secondary thing. Ego is, in a sense, a false thing, but it isn't necessarily bad. You have to start with Ego, and use Ego, and from there it gradually wears out, like a pair of shoes. But you have to use it and wear it out thoroughly, so it is not preserved. Otherwise, if you try to push Ego aside and start perfect, you may become more and more perfect in a rather one-sided way, but the same amount of imperfection is building up on the other side, just as creating intense light creates intense darkness as well.

Q. You mentioned that there are two basic forms of meditation—devotional practice, or trying to communicate with something higher, and the other one, which is simply awareness of what is—but this devotional practice still plays a part in Buddhism as well, and you have devotional chants and so on, but I am not quite sure how this comes in. I mean, the two appear to be different, so can they in fact be combined?

A. Yes, but the kind of devotional practice which is found in Buddhism is merely a process of opening, of surrendering the Ego. It is a process of creating a container. I don't mean to condemn the other kind of devotion, but if one looks at it from the point of view of a person who has an unskilful way of using that technique, then devotion becomes a longing to free oneself. One sees oneself as being very separate, and as being imprisoned and imperfect. One regards oneself as basically bad, and one is trying to break out. In other words the imperfection part of oneself is identified with "I" and anything perfect is identified with some external being, so all that is left is trying to get through the imprisonment. This kind of devotion is an overemphasized awareness of Ego, the negative aspect of Ego, although there are hundreds of variations of devotional practice in Buddhism, and there are many accounts of devotion to Gurus, or being able to communicate with the Guru, and of achieving the Awakened State of mind through devotion. But in these cases devotion is always begun without centralizing on the Ego. In any chants or ceremonies, for example, which make use of symbolism, or the visualization of Buddhas, before any visualization is created there is first a formless meditation, which creates an entirely open space. And at the end one always recites what is known as the Threefold Wheel: "I do not exist; the external visualization does not exist: and the act of visualizing does not exist"—the idea being that any feeling of achievement is thrown back to the openness, so one doesn't feel that one is collecting anything. I think that is the basic point. One may feel a great deal of devotion, but that devotion is a kind of abstract form of devotion, which does not centralize inwardly. One simply identifies with that feeling of devotion, and that's all. This is perhaps a different concept of devotion, where no center exists, but only devotion exists, whereas, in the other case devotion contains a demand. There is an expectation of getting something out of it in return.

Q. Is there not a great fear generated when we get to this point of opening up and surrendering?

A. Fear is one of the weapons of Ego. It protects the Ego. If one reaches the stage where one begins to see the folly of Ego, then there is fear of losing the Ego, and fear is one of its last weapons. Beyond that point fear no longer exists, because the object of fear is to frighten somebody, and when that somebody is not there, then fear loses its function. You see, fear is continually given life by your response, and when there is no one to respond to the fear—which is Ego loss—then fear ceases to exist.

Q. You are talking about the Ego as an object.?

A. In what sense?

Q. In the sense that it is part of the external environment.

A. Ego is, as I have already said, like a bubble. It is an object up to a point, because although it does not really exist—it is an impermanent thing—it in fact shows itself as an object more than actually being one. That is another way of protecting oneself, of trying to maintain Ego.

Q. This is an aspect of the Ego?

A. Yes.

Q. Then you can't destroy the Ego, or you would lose the power to recognize, the power to cognate.

A. No, not necessarily. Because Ego does not contain understanding, it does not contain any insight at all. Ego exists in a false way all the time and can only create confusion, whereas insight is something more than that.

Q. Would you say that Ego is a secondary phenomenon rather than a primary phenomenon?

A. Yes, very much so. In a sense Ego is wisdom, but Ego happens to be ignorant as well. You see, when you realise that you are ignorant, that is the beginning of the discovery of wisdom—it is wisdom itself.

Q. How does one decide in oneself whether Ego is ignorance or wisdom?

A. It is not really a question of deciding. It is simply that one sees in that way. You see, basically there is no solid substance, although we talk about Ego existing as a solid thing having various aspects. But in fact it merely lives through time as a continual process of creation. It is continually dying and being reborn all the time. Therefore Ego doesn't really exist. But Ego also acts as a kind of wisdom: when Ego dies, that is wisdom itself, and when Ego is first formulated that is the beginning of ignorance itself. So wisdom and Ego are not really separate at all. It seems rather difficult to define, and in a way one would be happier if there was clear-cut black and white, but somehow that is not the natural pattern of existence. There is no clear-cut black and white at all, and all things are interdependent. Darkness is an aspect of light and light is an aspect of darkness, so one can't really condemn one side and build up everything on the other. It is left entirely to the individual to find his own way, and it is possible to do so. It is the same for a dog who has never swum—if he was suddenly thrown in the water he could swim. Similarly, we have a kind of spiritual instinct in us and if we are willing to open ourselves then somehow we find our way directly. It is only a question of opening up and one doesn't have to have a clear-cut definition at all.

Q. Would you care to sum up the purpose of meditation?

A. Well, meditation is dealing with purpose itself. It is not that meditation is for something, but it is dealing with the aim. Generally we have a purpose for whatever we do; something is going to happen in the future, therefore what I am doing now is important—everything is related to that. But the whole idea of meditation is to develop an entirely different way of dealing with things, where you have no purpose at all. In fact meditation is dealing with the question of whether or not there is such a thing as purpose. And when one learns a different way of dealing with the situation, one no longer has to have a purpose. One is not on the way to somewhere. Or rather, one is on the way and one is also at the destination at the same time. That is really what meditation is for.

Q. Would you say, then, that it would be a merging with reality?

A. Yes, because reality is there all the time. Reality is not a separate entity, so it is a question of becoming one with reality, or of being in reality—not *achieving* oneness, but becoming identified with it. One is already a part of that reality, so all that remains is to take away the doubt. Then one discovers that one has been there all the time.

Q. Would it be correct to describe it as the realization that the visible is not reality?

A. The visible? Can you define a bit more?

Q. I am thinking of William Blake's theory of the merging of the observer with the observed, and the visible not being the reality at all.

A. Visible things in this sense are reality. There is nothing beyond nowness, therefore what we see is reality. But because of our usual way of seeing things, we do not see them exactly as they are.

Q. Would you say, then, that each person is an individual and must find an individual way towards that?

A. Well, I think that brings us back to the question of Ego, which we have been talking about. You see, there is such a thing as personality, in a way, but we are not really individuals as separate from the environment, or as separate from external phenomena. That is why a different approach is necessary. Whereas, if we were individuals and had no connection with the rest of things, then there would be no need for a different technique which would lead to oneness. The point is that there is appearance of individuality, but this individuality is based on relativity. If there is individuality, there must be also oneness as well.

Q. Yes, but it is the individuality that makes for oneness. If we weren't individuals we couldn't be one. Is that so?

A. Well, the word "individual" is rather ambiguous. At the beginning individuality may be overemphasized, because there are various individual aspects. Even when we reach the stage of realization there is perhaps an element of compassion, an element of wisdom, an element of energy and all sorts of different variations. But what we describe as an individual is something more than that. We tend to see it as one character with many things built onto it, which is a way of trying to find some sort of security. When there is wisdom, we try to load everything onto it, and it then becomes an entirely separate entity, a separate person—which is not so. But still there are individual aspects, there is individual character. So in Hinduism one finds different aspects of God, different deities and different symbols. When one attains oneness with reality, that reality is not just one single thing, but one can see from a very wide angle.

Q. If a student has a receptive mind and wishes to make himself at one with Nature, can he be taught how to meditate, or does he have to develop his own form?

A. Nature? How do you mean?

Q. If he wishes to study, can he accept other people's teaching, or can he develop them himself?

A. In fact it is necessary to receive oral instruction, oral teaching. Though he must learn to give before he can accept anything, he must learn to surrender. Secondly, he finds that the whole idea of learning stimulates his understanding. Also this avoids building up a great feeling of achievement, as though everything is 'my own work'—the concept of the self-made man.

Q. Surely that is not sufficient reason for going to receive instruction from a teacher, just to avoid the feeling that otherwise everything is self-made. I mean, in the case of someone like Ramana Maharshi, who attained realization without an external teacher, surely he shouldn't go and find a Guru just in case he might become big-headed?

A. No. But he is exceptional, that is the whole point. There is a way, it is possible. And basically no one can transmit or impart anything to anybody. One has to discover within oneself. So perhaps in certain cases people could do that. But building up on oneself is somehow similar to Ego's character, isn't it? One is on rather dangerous ground. It could easily become Ego's activity, because there is already the concept of "I" and then one wants to build up more on that side. I think—and this may sound simple, but it is really the whole thing—that one learns to surrender gradually, and that surrendering of the Ego is a very big subject. Also, the teacher acts as a kind of mirror, the teacher gives back one's own reflection. Then for the first time you are able to see how beautiful you are, or how ugly you are.

Perhaps I should mention here one or two small points about meditation, although we have already discussed the general background of the subject.

Generally, meditation instruction cannot be given in a class. There has to be a personal relationship between teacher and pupil. Also there are certain variations within each basic technique, such as awareness of breathing. But perhaps I should briefly mention the basic way of meditating, and then, if you want to go further, I am sure you could do so and receive further instruction from a meditation teacher.

As we have mentioned already, this meditation is not concerned with trying to develop concentration. Although many books on Buddhism speak of such practices as *Samatha* as being the development of concentration, I think this term is misleading in a way. One might get the idea that the practice of meditation could be put to commercial use, and that one would be able to concentrate on counting money or something like that. But meditation is not just for commercial uses, it is a different concept of concentration. You see, generally one cannot really concentrate. If one tries very hard to concentrate, then one needs the thought that is concentrating on the subject and also something which makes that accelerate further. Thus there are two processes involved and the second process is a kind of watchman, which makes sure that you are doing it properly. That part of it must be taken away, otherwise one ends up being more self-conscious and merely aware that one is concentrating, rather than actually being in a state of concentration. This becomes a vicious circle. Therefore one cannot develop concentration alone, without taking away the centralized watchfulness, the trying to be careful—which is Ego. So the *Samatha* practice, the awareness of breathing, is not concerned with concentrating on the breathing.

The cross-legged posture is the one generally adopted in the East, and if one can sit in that position, it is preferable to do so. Then one can train oneself to sit down and meditate anywhere, even in the middle of a field, and one need not feel conscious of having a seat or of trying to find something to sit on. Also, the physical posture does have a certain importance. For instance, if one lies down this might inspire one to sleep; if one stands one might be inclined to walk. But for those who find it difficult to sit cross-legged, sitting on a chair is quite good, and, in fact, in Buddhist inconography the posture of sitting on a chair is known as the *Maitreya asana,* so it is quite acceptable. The important thing is to keep the back straight so that there is no strain on the breathing. And for the breathing itself it is not a matter of concentrating, as we have already said, but of trying to become one with the feeling of breath. At the beginning some effort is needed, but after practicing for a while the awareness is simply kept on the verge of the movement of breath; it just follows it quite naturally and one is not trying particularly to bind the mind to breathing. One tries to feel the breath—outbreathing, inbreathing, outbreathing, inbreathing—and it usually happens that the outbreathing is longer than the inbreathing, which helps one to become aware of space and the expansion of breathing outwards.

It is also very important to avoid becoming solemn

and to avoid the feeling that one is taking part in some special ritual. One should feel quite natural and spontaneous, and simply try to identify oneself with the breath. That is all there is to it, and there are no ideas or analyzing involved. Whenever thoughts arise, just observe them *as thoughts,* rather than as being a subject. What usually happens when we have thoughts is that we are not aware that they are thoughts at all. Supposing one is planning one's next holiday trip: one is so engrossed in the thoughts that it is almost as though one were already on the trip and one is not even aware that these are thoughts. Whereas, if one sees that this is merely thought creating such a picture, one begins to discover that it has a less real quality. One should not try to suppress thoughts in meditation, but one should try to see the transitory nature, the translucent nature of thoughts. One should not become involved in them, nor reject them, but simply observe them and then come back to the awareness of breathing. The whole point is to cultivate the acceptance of everything, so one should not discriminate or become involved in any kind of struggle. That is the basic meditation technique, and it is quite simple and direct. There should be no deliberate effort, no attempt to control and no attempt to be peaceful. This is why breathing is used. It is easy to feel the breathing, and one has no need to be self-conscious or to try and do anything. The breathing is simply available and one should just feel that. That is the reason why technique is important to start with. This is the primary way of starting, but it generally continues and develops in its own way. One sometimes finds oneself doing it slightly differently from when one first started, quite spontaneously. This is not classified as an advanced technique or a beginner's technique. It simply grows and develops gradually.

13.

Meditation—Going Within

HELGA F. COZAD

Every great religion has an inner part and an outer, a spirit and a body, the knowledge of God, and its dogmas and rites. The Wisdom of God in a mystery is that knowledge which is known to the "perfect;" according to St. Paul. The "perfect" of St. Paul is the Self, "God within." This "God within" is not another entity, such as a spoon within a glass, or a being within a temple. To have "God within" in that manner is as much separateness as to have God without and apart. God within is divinity, oneness of being. And we reach this oneness of being by sinking in consciousness into the depths of our beings, beyond the human thought processes, beyond the body, the emotions, the passions, the mind, the reason—these all belong to man, but they are not man.

We need to go within daily. We need to meditate; as N. Sri Ram has said: "The Truth which we seek must be the Truth of direct experience . . . in which the distinction between subject and object has ceased to exist." Meditation is universal. In the book, *Footprints of Gautama the Buddha,* Marie Byles tells how the Master taught that merely to learn is not enough, merely to teach is not enough, and merely to ponder is not enough. "Such ones," said the Master, "if they neglect to go apart for meditation know not through actual experience and inner sight, the Goal Beyond, and they live not according to the Dhamma."

Jesus spoke of the kingdom of heaven being within, and to St. Peter he said, "Blessed art thou Simon Bar-jona: for flesh and blood hath not revealed it unto thee, but my Father which is in heaven . . . ." (Matt. 16:17) And when he taught his followers to pray he said, "But thou, when thou prayest, enter into thy closet, and when thou hast shut the door, pray to thy Father . . . ." (Matt. 6:6) The closet is the "within," the sanctuary of Self, that inner "Self" by which we have direct knowledge of God; the door we must shut is our physical senses, our emotions, our intellectual minds, that door of much noise; and to pray to thy Father, is the realization of our true Self, pure being, the "I AM" of Exodus 3:14. This is meditation.

This kind of meditation is more than a fundamental or even obvious study or contemplation of our nature and character; it is more than visualization. It must not be something done spasmodically to suit our emotions or pacify our frustrations. It must be a deliberate practice, an actual effort made daily that truly draws us within, and which is absolutely away from the concept of being apart from God, or a belief in separateness. It is a universal practice belonging equally to all great religions and is the sustaining life of every great religion. What is more, it may be possessed by any individual even outside any religious organization. To listen to the "still small voice" is to cease to be one's limited self and become the "Voice."

This meditation does not rely on intellectual processes. And when we find God first within the depths of our being we find Him everywhere, and within everyone; then we see the reality of brotherhood and

the oneness of being. Meditation is that part of religion which is a must for every student of Theosophy
if we are to express the glorious perfection and allness
of God. If Theosophy is not a religion, it certainly is
a deep responsibility. In Brazil, often the mistress
of the home will serve a large tray of many kinds of
fruits as a help to digestion of the food. This is how
I see Theosophy: An infinite tray of fruits of many
kinds, which the students of Theosophy, the keepers,
so to speak, have a responsibility to offer to the world
family of sentient beings to help digest this seemingly
torn world.

In his book, *The Way of the White Clouds,* Lama
Anagarika Govinda explains: "Due to our exclusive
concentration upon the cultivation of our intellectual
faculties we have neglected and, to a great extent,
lost our psychic sensitivity. Therefore to speak of
deities, Gods, Buddhas, and Bodhisattvas in any other
sense than that of poetical or metaphorical usage is
to expose oneself to the charge of superstition." And
we must not let that word "psychic" place us outside
of his statement, for it comes from the Greek word
for "soul," and, in this sense, "psychic sensitivity"
merely means "spiritual sensitivity." Madame Blavatsky teaches, in *Isis Unveiled,* that the three degrees
of knowledge are thought, perception, and envisage-
ment or intuition, and she speaks of "unveiled spiritual perception." This "perception" is enlightenment,
or a direct knowledge of God through meditation.
Then we find what she teaches to be the steps to the
Temple of Divine Wisdom: a clean Life, an open
Mind, a pure Heart, an eager Intellect . . .

There is a reality to spiritual power and purely
spiritual experience that is not below our intellectual
dignity, that is, unless we have the stamina to cling
to the thought that God is beneath our intellectual
dignity. Such spiritual experience, such spiritual

power, is a reality and cannot, must not be discarded as mere superstition or hallucination.

All religions have a single source, the Divine Wisdom. And we must seek and demonstrate that Divine Wisdom, which is based on a direct knowledge of God. Wisdom is a divine attribute which is latent within man. It unfolds as man progresses in the scale of evolution through experience of Life, Mind, Love, Truth, the manifestation of God. Divine Wisdom, for there is no "human wisdom," as a natural part of man's character which is the image or reflection of God. It is not human, nor even superhuman, based on the often false testimonies of the five physical senses. It is the pure and absolute reflection of God; and man realizes this Divine Wisdom in his experience only in as much and to that degree in which he is able to understand or perceive of God itself, man and the universe. The beginning is the awareness of Self; not through concepts of others, but through one's own experience of the perfection, the entirety, the allness of Self. Though our reading, our studies, our books are important, we must strive for balance and often stop to silence the physical processes, so to speak, to hear the explanation or instructions of God, the Father within. (An hour is not too much.)

Lama Govinda, in his book, has a beautiful explanation of what I understand "going within" to meditate means: "The one-pointedness of our consciousness is similar to the focalization of a lens; it can be utilised for bringing a particular object into focus, or for the focalization of consciousness itself by excluding any particular object and just letting consciousness rest in itself, integrated in its own awareness. In such a state one is not holding on to anything or concentrating on anything; the mind is completely free from object-awareness or from the interference of will-power or intellectual activity." That type of meditation helps one to "let the Father do it," in mental treatment.

Going within in meditation is not a mere turning inward of our thought processes. Human thoughts, whether inwardly or outwardly, in expressions are nevertheless "human thought processes." In my understanding, and founded on my own personal spiritual experiences during meditation, the Divine, being divine, is not aware of the human. Therefore one must stop the merely human to reach that absolute stillness. It is the stillness of our physical vibrations, so to speak, in which state of being we are no longer aware of ourselves as a physical body in a physical environment. It is in this "within" of meditation that the Entity, the "I AM" of Moses, the "still small voice" of Elijah, "the Father within" of Jesus, the "Buddha" of Gautama is reached. When we "return" from that meditation, we can say with Jacob, "for I have seen God face to face, and my life is preserved." (Gen. 32:30)

NOTES ON CONTRIBUTORS

MARIE BEUZEVILLE BYLES, of Australia, was
formerly a practicing lawyer and a keen tramper
and mountaineer. She is still active in work for
the conservation of wild life. When in India, she
gathered local color for her *Footprints of Gautama the Buddha* (now published in Quest
Books) which she wrote because there was no
account of the Buddha's ministerial life and
teaching. Her day-to-day experiences in meditation in Burma and Japan appear in her *Journey
into Burmese Silence* and *Paths to Inner Calm.*
She has also written *The Lotus and the Spinning
Wheel* and the Introduction to *A New Road to
Ancient Truth* by Tenko-San, the St. Francis of
Japan.

HELGA COZAD was born in Brazil but is now resident in the United States. She has for some time
been a student of comparative religions, is deeply committed to the spiritual basis of brotherhood, and regards herself as a "Buddhist Chris-
tion." Married, with a son and two daughters,
Mrs. Cozad still finds time to conduct study
groups of young people in the teaching of the ancient wisdom. She has made a special study of
meditation.

LAMA ANAGARIKA GOVINDA, who wrote his
first book on Buddhism at the age of 18, describes
himself as "an Indian national of European de-
scent and Buddhist faith, belonging to a Tibetan
Order and believing in the Brotherhood of

Man." He studied art, archaeology, and philosophy at three European universities and held a scholarship in archaeology which enabled him to travel extensively. His interest in Pali-Buddhism and monastic life led him to Ceylon and Burma, but he finally settled in India, expanded the sphere of his activities to Tibet, and became a member of the Tibetan Buddhist Order. He has held posts in various Indian universities and has had numerous exhibitions of his original paintings. During part of 1971 and 1972, he traveled and lectured in the United States and Canada and taught in the Perkins School of Theology of the Southern Methodist University, Dallas, Texas. He is the author of many books, notable among which are *Foundations of Tibetan Mysticism, The Way of the White Clouds,* and *The Psychological Attitude of Early Buddhist Philosophy.*

FELIX LAYTON was educated in England, Canada, and the United States, receiving the B. S. degree in physics at the University of Michigan and the M. A. degree at Stanford University. During World War II, he served as Major in the Royal Corps of Signals. For a number of years he was active in educational work at the International Headquarters of The Theosophical Society in Adyar, Madras, India, serving as Principal of the Besant Theosophical School and, at a later period, as Principal of the Olcott Harijan Free Schools. From 1966 to 1972 he was National Vice-President of The Theosophical Society in America, during which time he and Mrs. Layton were engaged in regional expansion work for the Society, lecturing and forming groups of members throughout the United States. He has lectured widely in India and other Asian countries, as well as in New Zealand, Australia, and Europe. He is the author, with Mrs. Layton, of the Quest Book, *Theosophy: Key to Understanding.*

SEETHA NEELAKANTAN has been a member of The Theosophical Society since 1940. She is a graduate in science and Sanskrit of Madras University in India and taught for 20 years in the Besant Theosophical High School at Adyar, the International Headquarters of The Theosophical Society. In 1957 she was appointed Librarian of the Adyar Library and Research Center. In 1968, at the invitation of the United States Section of the Society, she came to the national headquarters to develop the Oriental Section of the Olcott Library and Research Center. After two years at this post, she returned to her home in India, where she has resumed her duties in the Adyar Library and Research Center.

JOHN BRIAN PARRY, an accountant, is Finance Director of a large Australian firm. He holds a licentiate in Theology from the Australian College of Theology (Anglican) and is in Liberal Catholic Orders. For many years a member of The Theosophical Society in Australia, he has had a close interest in meditation and contemplation. He has had wide experience in the conducting of meditational retreats and in groups involved with various aspects of meditation.

JAMES S. PERKINS is International Vice-President of The Theosophical Society with headquarters at Adyar, Madras, India. Before appointment to that post, he served from 1945 to 1960 as National President of The Theosophical Society in America. A commercial artist by profession,

Mr. Perkins has given full time to the work of The Theosophical Society for many years. He is the author of numerous published works, his major books being *From Death to Rebirth* and *A Geometry of Space and Consciousness,* both illustrated with his own symbolic drawings and paintings. He is in demand as a lecturer in many countries and his writings appear frequently in theosophical journals.

SIMONS ROOF, professionally in advertising and public relations, is an honor graduate of the University of North Carolina and did graduate work at the University of Florida. During World War II he served as lieutenant and commanding officer of a minesweeper in the South Pacific. He spent more than two years in India in full time studies and writings, much of it in the verbal tradition of teaching on meditation. For about 18 months of that time, he lived in Kalimpong, near the Tibetan border. He has also studied Zen in Japan. Mr. Roof has taught classes in meditation for The Theosophical Society and other groups and has served as President of The Theosophical Society in Boston. He is the author of two books, *Journeys on the Razor-Edged Path* and *Greatness of Being.*

EDITH SCHLOSSER was born and educated in England, where she taught school for a number of years. Since coming to this country, she has followed a career in adult education in San Jose, California. She has served on the resident staff of The Theosophical Society in America in the Department of Education. Mrs. Schlosser has traveled and lectured widely and is a frequent contributor to theosophical and other journals.

V. WALLACE SLATER, B. Sc. (London) F.R.I.C., M.I. Chem. E., was professionally a chemical engineer and director of research in the chemical industry. He is a past General Secretary (President) of The Theosophical Society in England and served as Treasurer of that Section. He is a well known lecturer and author of books and articles on science as well as on Theosophy. Perhaps his best known books are *A Simplified Course in Hatha Yoga* and *Raja Yoga: A Simplified Course,* both in Quest editions.

I. K. TAIMNI, a native of India, now retired, was for many years a chemistry professor at Allahabad University, specializing in guided research in that field. A number of foreign technical journals have published his some fifty research papers in this discipline. In addition to his professional work, Dr. Taimni has long been interested in religion and philosophy and is the author of several books, the most recent being, *An Introduction to Hindu Symbolism, The Science of Yoga,* and *Man, God and the Universe.* A long-time member of The Theosophical Society, he served for a number of years as Director of the School of the Wisdom at the International Headquarters of the Society.

CHÖGYAM TRUNGPA, Rinpoche, a native of Tibet now living in the West, was known in his own country as a tulku and incarnate lama of high rank. At a very young age he was installed as the religious head and supreme abbott of a group of monasteries and underwent rigorous spiritual education and training. He was only 20 years of age when, at the time of the Chinese invasion, he managed to escape into India with some of his followers. The story of his life in Tibet, and of his escape from that country, is told in the book *Born in Tibet* as related to Esme Cramer Roberts in Oxford. Trungpa Tulku is associated with the Tail of the Tiger Buddhist Community and is presently holding a series of seminars and giving lectures in the United States.

HELEN V. ZAHARA is Chairman of the Department of Education of The Theosophical Society in America and Co-ordinator of special theosophical programs sponsored by the Kern Foundation, particularly the publication of Quest Books. She is a New Zealander by birth but came to the United States from Australia, where she had served for eight years as General Secretary (President) of the Society in that country, edited the theosophical journal published there, and conducted a weekly radio program. Miss Zahara is a certified accountant by profession but has devoted full time to The Theosophical Society since 1946, when she joined the staff at its International Headquarters at Adyar, Madras, India. She has traveled and lectured in more than 30 countries, and her name is a familiar one in theosophical journals throughout the world.

QUEST BOOKS

are published by The Theosophical
Society in America, a branch of
a world organization dedicated to the
promotion of brotherhood and the
encouragement of the study of religion,
philosophy, and science, to the end
that man may better understand
himself and his place in the universe.
The Society stands for complete
freedom of individual search and belief.
Quest Books are offered as a
contribution to man's search for truth.

Four additional Quest books
on the subject of meditation

CREATIVE MEDITATION AND MULTI-DIMENSIONAL CONSCIOUSNESS
by Lama Anagarika Govinda

A bridge between the metaphysics of the East and West based upon a life-long study and practice of Buddhism.

THE ART OF INNER LISTENING
by Jessie K. Crum

A basic, down-to-earth, first person account of the way to self-awareness. A self-help book.

CONCENTRATION
by Ernest Wood

Preliminary steps toward reaching a meditative state. Includes thirty-six physical and mental exercises.

MEDITATION — A PRACTICAL STUDY
by Adelaide Gardner

Specifically written for the Study and Training Committee of the Theosophical Society in England, now used widely for seminar work.